NICKY GUTTRIDGE

I'M JUST AN HCA

THE TRIALS, THE TEARS AND THE REWARDS OF WORKING AS A HEALTH CARE ASSISTANT

Throughout this book, I will use the following terms: orderly, auxiliary nurse, health care assistant (HCA), health care support worker (HCSW), carer, and support worker. These terms are interchangeable depending on the era. Job titles change with the times, but basically, all these people do similar jobs.

For obvious reasons, some names and places in this book have been changed.

Contents

Chapter

1 How it all started 1
2 Starting out 16
3 A change in career – becoming an agency HCA.......... 42
4 It takes all sorts.......... 61
5 Some shifts to remember.......... 67
6 Time to leave it all behind 134

Chapter 1

How it all started

HCA stands for Health Care Assistant. We are sometimes referred to as carers, and more recently the term Health Care Support Worker has been adopted. We are important members of a healthcare team who assist with the care of patients and so much more.

I feel that our work is not generally understood. Many people have never even heard of us and have no idea what the role entails.

A hospital HCA can do a very different job from one working in a GP practice. An HCA in a nursing home performs different tasks from one who works in a maternity ward and a HCSW (health care support worker) who works in a prison will have a very different role from the ones listed above. It is a job title that is shared by many and linked with many different establishments.

One thing that infuriates me is when others look down on us and assume all we do is wipe bums. There is so much more to it. I'm not quite sure why people focus on that. I find it a bit strange. This is why I decided to write this book. I just want to share my personal story of becoming, and working as, a Health Care Assistant.

Friends and family say to me 'How can you do that job, how can you deal with other people's poo, wee, sick etc?' but you just do it – it's your job. You don't think about it at the time. You may have a laugh and a joke about it with other HCAs and nurses, because they understand. If you have never worked in healthcare, it will be difficult for you to believe how gross it can be at times, and sometimes the smell is unbearable. It can at times be sad and upsetting too, but at the moment when you're in the middle of assisting with the person with personal care, you don't really think of that poor person whose mess you are cleaning up. It is only afterwards that you sometimes think how sad and upsetting it is. In many ways, you have to be strong because what we deal with and what we see is terribly distressing at times.

I read a sad article in the *Sunday Times Magazine* written by the writer Frederick Forsyth. He was recalling the sadness he felt about his father's decline into old age, and explained 'He was a very proud man, so the bodily malfunctions at the end profoundly humiliated him, almost crying with the embarrassment'.

I can relate to this because I have provided personal care to many people who could be shy and embarrassed.

Different eras and upbringings may change individuals' feelings about these difficult situations.

I'm certain every carer will agree with me when I say that we are often looked down upon. An ex-colleague of mine, Beverly, recalled a story from a few decades ago about an auxiliary nurse whom she worked alongside who had written an 'out of order' sign for a broken lift. She was reprimanded in front of some of her colleagues by a senior nurse who told her 'You're not qualified enough to write that.' Can you imagine hearing that nowadays? This just proves that even years ago people doing this job were being undervalued.

A medical student was quoted as saying, 'Working as an HCA (from what I've heard) is one of the toughest, most demoralising jobs out there in the health profession, and yet there's so much to be learned from it'. (internurse.com)

When I meet another HCA, I feel there is a certain connection. You think they will understand exactly where you're coming from, because you too clean poo, sick, blood, and wee up for a living. Oh yes, and false teeth, don't forget those. Maybe you don't get that in quite the same way within other professions.

HCAs who work in hospitals are expected to do a lot of nursing tasks. This was certainly true of me when I was employed by a nursing agency. I was doing more and more nursing tasks than I ever used to do when I first started work in the hospitals. Especially if we have done the NVQ 3 National Vocational Qualification for example taking and recording blood pressures and general observations, doing the blood sugar results for diabetic patients, or taking Venflons out (those little plastic tubes or cannulas which are inserted in your hand when you have had surgery, to allow intravenous medication). I did not complete my phlebotomy training, so I was never qualified to take patients' blood, but many of my HCAs colleagues do. The courses were hard to get onto back in the 1990s.

As HCAs in hospitals, we are part of the whole medical team. When the crash team are called for, we also run to assist, and we experience the same adrenalin rush as the rest of the team. It didn't happen very often for me, but it was a good buzz when it did.

Nursing Standard magazine reported recently: 'A new workforce of healthcare assistants (HCAs) are starting to take on some of the work that nurses used to do'. In the last decade, things have changed for hospital HCAs and if you show competence, experience and common sense, the trained nurses (well, some of them!) are happy for us to take a little of their heavy workload off them.

I liked this quote that I found in the Nursing Standard: 'Nurses' decisions to delegate work to HCAs depend on their confidence in the individual and not on whether they have NVQs or not'. (NS 12 Oct 2006). Even though the above quote was written seventeen years ago, I still think it stands true today.

I enjoyed the nursing side of the job along with the caring side. However, this next quote, from David Salvage, is very true: 'The basic HCA job used to be to assist a nurse in patient care, why has this changed? Is it because HCAs are less expensive?'

I think he hit the nail on the head. Is it not what everything seems to be about in the last two decades – money and cutbacks? Unfortunately, this is still going on today in the health industry. More for less, from everyone employed in this sector. Since Covid hit us all, more and more staff have been just quitting or moving on, leaving behind the qualifications they have worked hard for, as it is less stressful and more pay to work in a different less stressful environment.

When I went into this job as a health care assistant, as it slotted into my lifestyle and family commitments, I also felt that in a majority of cases, the reason for a lot of people doing this sort of work is that like me, they came out of school with no qualifications. Or very few, and therefore like me this was one of the jobs suitable at that time (1992). If you wanted a 'care' job it tended to be an easy way into employment to work in the care homes, nurseries or play schools that you went to work in at sixteen and it also fits in with working parents.

When I first started in the role it required no qualifications. Almost anyone could get a job as a care assistant in a residential or nursing home. I think this changed around 2015 or 2016 with some reporting body or high-up person deciding care staff needed a Care Certificate like a BTEC, NVQ, or health and social care.

In the past I always felt slightly embarrassed when asked 'What do you do then?' and always replied 'I am *just a* carer' Some people know we are classed as one of the lowest-paid occupations. I found myself saying 'I'm going to do my nurse training' and saying things to justify why I was an HCA. Always when people say to me 'You're a nurse aren't you'? I say 'no, I'm just a...'

I have always had huge respect for nurses because they have done medical training and I have worked with many nurses and seen first-hand how hard and stressful the job can be for them. It's not a nice feeling when you do a job that certain people look down upon. I was once at the dentist, and he asked me if I was a nurse and I found I was saying it again '*I'm just an...'*.

I decided to stop saying *I'm just an...'* and to be proud of myself, so I changed and replied, 'I am an HCA'. Often you go on to explain what that is, as so many people still don't recognise the role. That makes me sad and says a lot really, because there are thousands of us, and we just aren't seen or recognised. Maybe it has taken Covid to make certain people aware. I hope so.

I would like to thank Ed Balls, who starred in a BBC2 programme called 'The Care Crisis'. It was a brilliant insight into what care staff actually do in a health care role.

Ed got stuck in and did the job, and massive respect to him for doing that. I recommend you watch it.

When I worked as an HCA, I liked going to work. I enjoyed the patient contact it gave me, but I also liked to walk out of the building and forget about my job on the way home, albeit not on time on many occasions. Also caring, like nursing, is a job which will never end. A forever job, if you want it. But this means many staff cannot just look at the finish time and go. It's just part and parcel of being employed by the medical industry.

When I worked for the Ambulance Service for a short spell, I found that whilst dressed in their uniform I was afforded much more respect than when I was dressed in a carer's uniform. It's shocking how judgemental people can be.

How this book came about

I saw and learned so much working as an HCA, particularly when I was employed via a nursing agency. I wish now I had made notes from every shift. Even though some shifts were not that eventful, there is always something you can recall. Whilst working for the agency I had many significant incidents, which have left a huge impact on me, and is the main reason for wanting to share my experiences and reflections. One incident upset me a lot, to the point where I couldn't get off to sleep afterwards. It was a night shift I worked with a not-very-nice person. I refuse to call her a carer. I took the hard decision to report her, and she was the only person I have ever reported. She was nasty with her words and spoke to the residents in a harsh way. Something I saw her do unsettled me, and I just couldn't go to sleep after the shift. She was a downright bully, in fact out of all the HCAs and nurses I have worked with she was the harshest and mean-spirited. That shift I spent with her also changed me, and I decided to be stronger and try and say something or call them out if anything like this happened again. My manager rang the home to tell them how she had behaved. From that shift onwards I started to make notes, which have become this book.

I did witness another act of cruel behaviour somewhere else; it was an Easter Sunday many years ago. I don't really want to elaborate on what happened, but by this time I had grown a thick skin and tried hard not to let anyone intimidate me. I told a few fellow carers that doing a job that did not involve care work would be much more suited to them. Hopefully, I made them think a little bit about how they were behaving.

This incident happened in one of the bathrooms of the establishment and it involved the person I was working alongside again. As before, I refused to call her a carer. She ended up getting wet with a threat of being reported. The rest of that shift was extremely strained and when I got home, I rang my Nana for a chat. I didn't tell Nan what had happened, I just wanted to hear her voice to reassure myself that I had done the right thing in soaking that bitch.

Of course, I did used to think about doing nurse training many times and was told on a few occasions by some nurses whom I worked alongside that I would have been a brilliant nurse, which was always nice to hear. I did take the entrance exam when I was seventeen but failed. I really should have done it instead of my Social Work and Welfare Studies degree, but sometimes your path in life takes you in other directions.

We all have different roles to play to different people, mainly our close relatives and friends, and we all share a few of the titles we hold. Your family and friends may never actually see you at work and may only have a vague idea of what your job entails. They know where you work and what your job title is and often listen to your moans and groans, but it's only really your colleagues that understand what you do day to day. Maybe that's why many people form strong friendships with co-workers, as I luckily did.

Most of the care staff I worked with over the years were good kind people who were game for a laugh. I have also worked with people who in my opinion should not have been in care work, as some just didn't care.

My time as an HCA with a nursing agency sent me to many different medical establishments. You name it, I have probably worked there: nursing homes, residential homes, young disabled units, secure psychiatric units, plus almost every ward in two large NHS hospitals, an elderly community hospital, two private medical hospitals, one private cosmetic hospital, and a couple of GP surgeries! I do feel lucky to have worked in some beautiful old buildings that wouldn't be out of place in a BBC period drama series – they certainly have a very different feel to them from a purpose-built establishment. They can be spooky and grand and they must hold many secrets and memories. I always felt like Lady Mary from Downton Abbey walking down the grand staircases of these buildings, although with my strong Lancashire accent and uniform with Crocs or trainers, I wouldn't exactly hardly look, or sound, the part!

I was sent to a hospital that had once been a Victorian workhouse, an institution intended to provide work and shelter for poverty-stricken people who had no means to support themselves. Unfortunately I slept in. I opened my eyes and went into a panic when I saw that the clock read quarter to seven, as I was rostered to start at seven. I jumped out of bed, got into my uniform, and jumped on my Z400 motorbike and zoomed off. I just made it on time. In the rush I had not eaten anything or put any food in my rucksack. All shift my tummy was rumbling and a lovely cleaner heard it. I explained my morning to her, and she got me a cheese sandwich and a brew. I was so grateful. We had a great chat about the old building and I said how I loved these establishments. She advised me to go to the corridor on the ground floor and look at all the pictures on the wall of the workhouse and the sad faces of the people in those photos. I wondered if there were any old workhouse ghosts there. I am open-minded about clairvoyants and spirits.

I was working a night shift in a grand old establishment and dawn was just breaking, so some time around four am I went up to the top floor to answer a buzzer. As I was coming down I stopped to look out of the window on the landing. It overlooked the vast park that had once belonged to the home in the olden days and I looked out across the wide lawn. It was a misty morning, and I saw a horse and carriage going across the lawn. I was a bit freaked out and ran downstairs to tell my colleagues what I had seen. The non-believers sniggered and told me I had been hallucinating, while others told me their ghost stories or sightings or odd spooky things that had happened to them, all very interesting. When my shift finished, I took some time to go and have a look at the photographs. That building was demolished and is now a housing estate.

If you have patience, are warm, friendly, and respectful, and love helping other people, then this may be a job for you. I have listened to many stories from nurses and HCAs over the years They all have a mixture of stories to tell, some funny, some sad, some truly awful, and some that most definitely don't need to be repeated. I have found myself in many sad and interesting situations, and picked up some tales from co-workers along the way.

Being an HCA can be emotionally and physically exhausting, and some shifts can be very challenging. For many years I worked unsocial hours for low wages. Sadly it still is a notoriously low-paid job and I think a lot of employers still only pay the minimum wage. This is such a shame, as many great staff move on from the job due to the low rate of pay. If you ran a poll and asked any nurse or carer if they are underpaid and understaffed at work, I would bet they would all answer yes. Only now am I finally earning a good wage after thirty-seven years of trying hard to better myself and can finally afford to buy myself nice things instead of having to always shop in the cheaper shops, always looking for a bargain at Christmas, and watching my wages disappear very quickly.

Working shifts in many caring establishments is extremely hard work, with long and busy day shifts or finishing a late shift to go back to do the early shift. A few of my friends still don't get to find out what their Christmas work pattern will be on the run-up to the festivities, so they can't just book a weekend away in their diary as most of the time they will have a shift.

A lot of crappy shift patterns can leave you completely drained and exhausted, and then you have to go back and do it all again. We know being employed within healthcare is not a nine-to-five job. We accept that we will miss a lot of social occasions, as do all shift workers. I remember working a night shift one Saturday night, and my husband Andy was dropping me off before going to meet some friends for a Guinness, as it was St Patrick's Day. I was so fed up and really wanted to go and meet our friends for a good old Saturday night. But that's the deal when you are a shift worker, especially when you are employed as relief staff, accept the shift offered and honour it. It stings a bit sometimes when you miss gatherings of family and friends.

When there is a full moon, a night shift can become very eventful. We use the term 'sundowning' to describe a person who acts very strangely during the night. Sundowning is a symptom of Alzheimer's disease and other forms of dementia. It's also known as 'late-day confusion'. If someone you care for has dementia, their confusion and agitation will often get worse in the late afternoon and evening. I have witnessed this a lot.

Night shifts are such a drain and a lot of us do them to fit in with family life. I never stayed in bed long enough during the day to make up for the lost hours. I had two children under six when I was doing most of my night shifts.

I do advise a bar of chocolate and an energy drink to help see you through, any time from 2 am to 4 am when the tiredness kicks in.

I wrote the following after being awake for thirty-six hours, and reading it back I think it's quite funny, but it just shows how lack of sleep can make you feel.

I can't decide what's worse, a raging hangover or the extreme tiredness that I am feeling at this moment. I've got a horrible feeling in the pit of my stomach - is it an ache or hunger? I can't tell. A slight headache that is just there at the back of my head has been there since about four am this morning when the tiredness hits you like a high-speed head-on collision.

The SAS keep captives awake as a means of punishment and I can see why. I would say or do anything right now just to be able to go to sleep.

My irritability is toppling like a lid on a pan of boiling potatoes. I have a huge guilty feeling hanging over me because I haven't taken my three-year-old to parent and toddler swim class today, something that is normally a regular occurrence for a Thursday and because of the tiredness making me an emotional wreck I have just cried because of this. Not to mention I attended Toddler Group this morning, which is not the quietest of places at the best of times, never mind when you haven't been to bed the night before.

I worked with another stranger again last night, this is just one of the hardest bits about being an agency worker, never being part of a team. I had to stay awake today because I could not find anyone to look after my little one.

I wrote that about 9 pm after being awake for far too long. I know from talking with friends and colleagues that I am not alone in working nights, then staying awake when I go off duty.

Angela, a friend who is a trained nurse, also works night shifts, at one of the big NHS hospitals near to where we live. She has three daughters and was also at a toddler group that same morning, and she was off to work that evening to do the night shift. Angela and I tidied all the toys away and locked up and were the last two to leave.

When I was working as an HCA, I always felt I was given more respect by the qualified nurses who had worked their way up from the HCA ranks. A lot of student nurses supplement their incomes whilst studying by working shifts as carers or HCAs in nursing homes or hospitals. They understand what it is like to be the lowest-paid member of staff. They have walked in our shoes. This is still true today, as some people see us as unskilled. No wonder we get angry, upset and frustrated with this, especially when Covid hit us all. Healthcare staff stepped up as they always have done, but they did so much more when lockdown arrived. With the restrictions that were implemented, loved ones could not visit their own family members who lived in a healthcare home any more. Carers stepped up bigger than ever before and did what they have done for years – they cared.

We clap for carers – but still pay them a shite wage. It's a good job, so many caring staff are dedicated to their relentless roles even though they are drained, angry, upset, frustrated, and yet still undervalued. Ask Ed Balls, he now knows how hard it is.

Chapter 2

Starting out

In my mid-teens, I was sent on work experience from school. I think I just made it up when I told my teacher I would like a job helping people, as you had to say something, and at age fourteen or fifteen, I had not the foggiest idea what I wanted to do. To be honest I was one of those kids at school in the eighties who was dumped in the lowest sets or seated at the 'thick table'. So, let's face it, I wasn't going to become a brain surgeon.

Some young schoolchildren know what they want to be when they 'grow up' and stay focused, work hard and achieve their dreams, but I was never one of them. However, I have worked hard and given my best since obtaining my first job aged fourteen. I have been put down on a few occasions by a couple of people who have said negative things to me over the years, I learned that my mum was told when I was little that I had a learning difficulty, so all in all I am quite proud of myself to be where I am today.

I was sent across the road from school to a place called Charnley Fold. Back then it was a Lancashire County Council-run residential home, and the residents were elderly and had a variety of needs. I don't really remember much about my time there, just bits and pieces, like the smell of lunch cooking, the layout of the place and making a bed, and feeding an old lady.

I do remember going along with another carer to bathe an elderly chap. This was the first naked person I had seen outside my family, bearing in mind I was only fourteen or fifteen years old, and it was a man! I remember at the time being totally embarrassed and slightly mortified. I am now much older and wiser and I can smile and remember feeling good that we made this chap feel clean and cared for and it made me feel worthy and competent. I was happy to help with this task. Looking back, I think that was the day when I realised I did want a career in helping others.

Charnley Fold is still there, but it is not a nursing home anymore.

Caring and nursing are in my blood. My Grandma Eileen, who I miss tremendously, was also an HCA, but they were known back then as orderlies. She worked at Preston Royal Infirmary around the time when my brother Joe, sister Lucy and I were born in the 1970s.

Also, my mum's sister, Auntie Bon, is a trained nurse. She has worked at her place of employment for many years and has recently been given a long-service award.

They spoke about her amazing sense of humour, which runs in our family.

I had forgotten about my time here, and it only came back to me when I started writing this book. I realized that this was my first step on a long and winding road that would see me working in health care to this day. Since then, I have gained years of hands-on experience, attended lots of courses and gained numerous certificates, and I still feel very strongly about the way carers are treated.

I left school in 1988 with some terrible grades for subjects like 'Science for everyday life', which my children think is hilarious. Thankfully after my work experience my mind was made up – I had decided that I *would* like a career that involved caring. I had wanted to care for babies and little ones at that time, but my career path took me the opposite way.

College and placements

So off I went to Tuson College, as it was known then, and completed a course titled 'Family and Community Care'. I wanted to study caring for children, but I had left it a bit too late and there were no spaces for me so I was placed on this course instead.

I think this course was cobbled together to cater for the school leavers who didn't fit anywhere else in the college. They had us doing all sorts, cooking, dressmaking, how to make a bed... it was a weird course, looking back, but it gave me my first qualification in care work. It also gave me a lifelong friend, which in my opinion is worth more than any qualification. Hazel and I were both sixteen. I soon learned she was one day older than me, so an Aries and almost the same birthday. We were destined to be best buddies. After a few years of friendship I was in my attic and looking through my baby book. My mum had kept the newspaper clipping from the advertisement of my birth and as I read the advert for the baby above I realised it was Hazel. She is one in a million and is my go-to person.

We had such a laugh on this course and mucked about for two years solid. We were based on the third floor and students were forbidden to use the lift, so of course what did we do every day? We regularly got caught and told off for this by Miss J, who made us go back down the stairs and up again. We had no respect for the rules.

One day we decided to skive off, so Hazel and I, with two others, jumped on a train to Blackpool. We had a brilliant day and had a ride on the beach donkeys and ice creams. I bet Miss J also had a brilliantly peaceful day without us. Recently I found some old photos from our time on the course, and we laughed so much reminiscing. Hazel bumped into Miss J recently and she remembered us – I bet she did! I must thank her for being such a god teacher for us crazy sixteen-year-olds.

Hazel and I have done okay in life and have gone

through many experiences together with our loyal husbands and kids. We always talk about writing a book about the ups and downs of bringing kids up, so watch this space. Hazel also did a care job once or twice and has a funny story to tell about giving a lady a morning cuppa and a wash and then discovering she was at the wrong house, so that job didn't last long for her. The lady was saying 'this is so lovely of you, I don't normally get this treatment'. Hazel had been told the lady she was meant to be assisting was slightly confused, so she carried on scrubbing her clean. It was only when she left and looked at her house number it clicked – she was supposed to be next door!

During the two-year course, I was sent on three placements. The first was to a pre-school. As I wanted to work with children this was a fantastic opportunity for me, and I loved it. I was so excited to look after the little ones in a happy place. I took in some dough and tins to make each toddler a mini loaf, and they were thrilled with the end results. A few of them had taken a little nibble before they proudly showed them off to whoever collected them at home time.

I got the dough from my Saturday job at that time at a local bakery close to where I grew up. The owners were so lovely and were happy to help me. It was a family-run place, and this was my first paid job. I used to start at 4 am, and I worked my way up to head Saturday girl and absolutely loved it there. I soon mastered my seven times table as the bread buns were seven pence each. Everyone was so kind to me. One of the bakers used pick me up at 4 am and drive me to work, which was such a bonus as it meant my parents didn't have to get up to take me. I used to finish around midday and skip home with my wage, then go straight to town and spend it in HMV on a rock single or a poster of Jon Bon Jovi. I still smile and remember the delicious smell of freshly baked bread when I pass the place where it once stood.

The second placement was a school for children with learning difficulties and challenging behaviour. It was a bit different from playing being Mrs Hovis with the little ones! It was certainly an eye opener. I was quite shocked at their behaviour. They seemed to sense my fear and kept trying to hit me.

The final placement I was sent to before completing my college course was at a nursing home, luckily for me quite close to where I lived. Being short staffed, like many nursing homes, they offered me a full-time position. As my course was nearly finished complete, I accepted their offer. I also felt that it would be good to get paid for doing the job that I had just done for free on placement for two weeks. It was not much, but better than nothing. This was 1990, when I was 18 years old. It was the start of my working life in healthcare.

My generation back then was frightened of questioning our elders and just did as we were asked without questioning anything. It was seen as very rude to question things, so we just put up with things that didn't seem fair. My children, who are both now around this age, are allowed to question managers and terms and conditions and are not afraid to speak up and stick up for themselves, and I think this is a good thing

Lovely memories with colleagues who became lifelong friends

After nine months of working in the nursing home, I felt confident enough to apply for the same role at a slightly smaller nursing home even nearer to where I lived. They offered me a position and I worked there for seven years, although I left for four months to work for Lancashire Ambulance Service, working in patient transport. Let's just say it was not for me. However, I got through the tough interview process, and I got to drive an ambulance – no blue lights, just a patient transport one. That's something that not many people can say.

I loved working in this nursing home and sometimes wish I had a time machine to take me back there. I consider that to be the best job I ever had. That's where I met Carole, Pam and Maggie, who have become lifelong best friends. I love them so much and when we get together, we always reminisce and laugh about the fun times and lovely residents we cared for at the nursing home. Thirty years later we still struggle to get the four of us together, as two of the gang still do shift work. Pam, who is the best carer I have ever worked with, has recently worked seven weekends in a row. She has the knack of being able to coax any resident into a bath even if they were adamant that they don't really need one, and she is always so caring and compassionate with everyone. She even washed my hair one time after I had accidentally dipped it into a commode when I was bending and twisting to wipe a bum, and my long ponytail went in the bucket. Luckily there was only wee in it. I was known by a couple of residents as 'donkey's tail,' as my hair was long and plaited at that time.

A patient's relative once said to Carole that she knew Pam had been on the early shift, as her mum had her hair done nicely, had her bracelet on and a touch of eye shadow. She knew Pam was the only one who would take the time to do this for her mum, and she was so thankful.

One day Pam stitched me up. She had emptied a commode for one of our blind residents, who stayed in his room all the time as he was most comfortable in his surroundings and was happy listening to the telly. Pam decided to give his bucket a good soak in bleach. Donald had sat down to have a number two, but being blind he didn't know the bucket was not in position. He soon realised and went ballistic, so she turned his buzzer off and said to me, 'Donald is asking for you'. I was on my hands and knees cleaning it up listening to him going crazy and

I couldn't stop laughing. I was thinking of all the ways I would get her back.

Carole was and still is the funny one and always makes us laugh so much. She told me a story about when she worked for a care agency. She was at a rest home and the staff said to her at lunch time when Carole was going to start serving the residents, 'Carole, we do Grace first,' and Carole said 'Which one is she?'

Maggie just spent the whole time laughing, and being so lovely with the residents, she was always tidying and cleaning up.

Another friend for life I met there is Shelagh. In my eyes she is the best-trained nurse I have ever worked with, and I have worked with so many. We are still good friends to this day. We worked at this nursing home together, then met up again years later at a hospital where we were both employed and did a good few night shifts together.

We had a brilliant team in this nursing home. I still see most of them knocking around where we live and like to see what they are all up to on the socials. Sadly, we have said goodbye to some of the team, as they have now passed away. We all worked well together and had some good laughs. I remember laughing so much about this next memory. In most homes there are old gentlemen who think they are in a Carry On film. Pam and I were washing a chap one day after he had wet himself. We always used to try to get the residents to wash their genitalia themselves if they were capable. This chap was having none of it and said to Pam 'Come on, I pay my money I want the service!' He was holding onto his zimmer frame and thrusting his groin towards Pam. She was a bit cross and told him off. I nearly wet *my* groin laughing so much.

We used to say that if you didn't laugh you would have cried. In this line of work, we do see some very sad, upsetting, degrading sights. It's always sad when one of the people who you have formed a relationship with and cared for with love and compassion passes away, and of course when caring for the elderly this happens quite often. We always used to try and attend the funeral if we could. I think I had been to about ten funerals before I was twenty-five.

My first experience of 'laying out' a dead patient is also quite vivid in my memory. Thankfully I was working with a very lovely caring nurse Pat. It's very strange walking into a room where there is a dead body on the bed, still warm having only just passed away. It was a lovely summer day and I remember Pat opening the window to 'let the spirit out'. I thought this was part and parcel of the process for years, but when I went to work at other establishments and they didn't 'let the spirit out' I realised that Pat was religious and attended church quite often, and this was one of her beliefs. However, I did like her way of letting the spirit go and I always did this whenever I was doing this task.

It was mysterious entering this woman's bedroom after she had passed. It had been her room for a few years, and after we had done what we had to do, within a day or two the next person would be settling in this room. I suppose this is part of the circle of life.

The bedroom curtains were closed, and the daylight was shining through. Pat explained to me that when a person has died the healthcare staff clean the body, change the bedclothes and prepare the body for their family to come and say their goodbyes. I remember washing and changing this person, someone's loved one, explaining to her what we were doing, talking as if they were still alive. We were treating her with respect and dignity. I remember being a bit freaked out when we moved the body and the wind escaped, producing a burp. I panicked a bit. thinking 'oh my goodness she's not dead after all'. Pat explained that it happens a lot – it's just the last bit of gas releasing from the body. You do get used to it.

I have laid many patients out over the years, but I will always remember my first one and I was glad it was Pat who taught me how do it with so much dignity and respect.

I'll just share with you a quote regarding death that I thought was excellent and sums it all up really: 'Forceps, epidurals, and caesareans ease our passage into the world. What is there to ease our paths from it?' (Quoted in *Your Ultimate Choice* 1992. P12)

Of course, when you are caring for the elderly, it's inevitable that you will be dealing with dying and death. For many people who have lost loved ones the grieving process begins before death has occurred.

Watching a loved one suffer is not nice to experience and can be very distressing. Most of us have lost loved ones, and in my case it was my mum Janet, who was only thirty-nine years of age. And guess where I was on my mum's last ever Christmas Day? Yes, I was working a bloody early shift caring for other families' loved ones.

This is the poem my mum wrote when she had lost the use of her legs and knew she was dying.

As I sit here day after day
I wonder if I'll fade away,
I wonder if, I wonder when,
I wonder if my life will end.
My family, my friends, I love so much,
Sometimes I muddle things which are Double Dutch.
I pray to God day after day
If he's finished with me to take me away.
The thing I'd love would be to walk,
But all I do is sit and talk.
The TV I watch day in day out
If I had the strength I'd throw it out.
Friends come and go but here I sit until to bed I go.
If I had my life to live again,
Knowing now what I know then
I'd care for people and give love more,
Because you never know when it's time to go.

Another poignant memory in history was Princess Diana's funeral. Yes, I was working an early shift that day too. Most of us were in the sitting room watching this emotional day unfold on the telly and then we heard 'Please can you take me to the toilet?'

One episode that will stay with me forever is the day that a male resident, Bob, got one of his balls stuck in the drainage hole of his bath chair. We dried him off and wound the bath chair up and out of the bath. We half-dressed him and almost finished the bathing process. All we had to do was dry his bum, pull his pants up and off he could go for a cup of tea and a rest. So 'one two three, stand'. One of us was on each side of Bob to assist him to stand. 'Ooooooooh!' Bob cried, and we stopped. Bob just said 'Ball!'

Word spread quickly that Bob had got one of his testicles stuck in the bath chair. All the staff gathered outside the bathroom worrying about old Bob, the kitchen staff offered frozen peas to try and shrink the testicle so it would pop back through. We tried KY jelly, but nothing was working. Bob did not seem to be upset or distressed about this at all. We got him a cup of tea and of course we had to telephone for the family, plus the ambulance and fire service. When the fire and ambulance staff assessed the situation, they all left the room with looks of horror on their faces especially the male staff, sympathising with Bob, who was sat there half-dressed sipping his cup of tea.

The fire crew were just about to get their cutting equipment (for the bath chair, not Bob's testicle) when it decided to pop back through the hole in the chair. We all breathed a sigh of relief. Bob was ok and never complained about this episode, but we kept a close eye on him and his slightly bruised ball! I think the story made it into one of the nursing or caring magazines. I heard the design of these bath seats was changed as apparently, this was not the first time it had happened. We were all told to put a towel onto the holey seats to prevent any more balls getting stuck before equipment was changed.

If you Google 'ball stuck in bath chair' there is a similar story of a fella and an Ikea chair. Also, season one, episode two of Station Nineteen is very similar. It's on Disney Plus if you want to watch it. You don't see any balls, just a warning for the more squeamish amongst you.

Another memory of laughing till I cried was when Edith was convinced someone was stealing her chocolate. She decided to roll up some of her poo and put it in the Turkish delight box and asked Maggie to pass her the box and take one for herself. The joke is still going strong to this day: 'does anyone fancy a Turdish Delight?' Thankfully Maggie declined Edith's offer.

On the late shift it was the carers' job to do the laundry. I remember on one occasion when rushing I managed to put a red underskirt in with a load of whites by mistake. When we went to empty the machine, all the undies were pink. I kept my mouth shut and swore Carole to secrecy, but I will take this opportunity to apologise to the patients whose white undies turned pink. Whoops!

Sometimes trying to get a resident into the bath was a chore - I think they just couldn't be bothered with the whole rigmarole. We had a chap who had turned back into a lazy teenager who did not like to wash, and one day Maggie and I persuaded him to have a bath. He was saying 'don't put my trousers in the wash' and we thought he was just being a bit unhygienic, but it turned out he had two hundred pounds in the pocket! No one knew this, not even his son, who we called to update about this discovery. No wonder he didn't want to take them off. Most old folks have tissues or Werther's Originals in their pockets, not two hundred quid! Good job Brenda checked the pockets before we laundered them!

Mealtimes are always such a busy and time-consuming task in any care home, as we need to get them all into the dining room at the same time. With most of the residents having disabilities, we had to offer a lot of assistance, and it was like Wacky Races with wheelchairs, zimmer frames and three wheelers. Often residents have a sleep after lunch, and sometimes staff can benefit from a nap too.

One day I was doing a bit of tidying up with a dustpan and brush when someone shouted for my help as a resident had almost had a fall. As I dashed off to help, I placed the dustpan onto the table without thinking and one of the residents started helping himself to the extra helping of brushed-up floor bits! I caught the same confused resident sucking on a vinegar bottle the day after. It's sad to see confused residents doing these things because of one of the many medical conditions that can make an elderly person act in such ways. Most staff members have been punched, nipped, scratched or swore at. Carole got a punch in the face one day when she had just returned from the dentist. I will never forget it. We had just sat the resident on the toilet, when bam! She was really hurt. It was awful seeing my friend get a right hook. We know the residents can't help it, but it still hurts.

Another time we took some of the residents on a day trip out to a lovely posh café. Our vinegar-sucking resident was sucking on a tablecloth and others made such a mess with crumbs and spillages. On the way out, one of the residents lost his incontinence pad, and shook it out of his trouser leg. I remember looking back as I scooped the sodden pad off the pavement and seeing two waitresses looking traumatised. But this was just everyday life to us carers.

One morning a resident of ours was walking along the corridor very smartly dressed in a shirt, tie and blazer. He had his socks held up with little sock suspenders and very clean and smart shoes. As he walked by us, he said 'morning ladies' and we all burst out laughing because he was wearing no undies or trousers, and it was such a sight to see as he walked by totally unaware of what was missing. Some may think it was a bit mean for us to be laughing at this, but we soon sorted him out and it was funny. He was a lovely man and he had become elderly and confused. The man he had once been had gone. He laughed with us when we steered him, with a towel around his waist, to his room and helped him complete his outfit for the day, but at any point of the day he may remove the top or bottom half again!

The day we got our first minibus was a fab occasion. I remember it being an old-fashioned rickety white monstrosity. Pam and I were given the task of taking a few of our residents for a little ride out in the minibus for the afternoon. We set off, Pam driving, and we had a singsong, 'Daisy, Daisy, give me your answer do' or something similar. As we were driving, I said 'Shelagh [the best nurse ever] lives along here, let's show her the new vehicle and say hello'. We parked up and I knocked. Shelagh was so pleased to see us all and insisted we all went in for a cuppa and a digestive, so we offloaded our residents and aided them into Shelagh's home. It was so lovely of her to invite these incontinent residents into her beautiful home to sit on her Laura Ashley settee!

When we returned to the home slightly late for tea, Matron was fuming with us as we had been gone all afternoon and of course that had left them without two of the best (!) staff. She said how inappropriate it was taking the residents into Shelagh's home. We bowed our heads, apologised and insisted all the residents had had a great afternoon outing, but she didn't see it like that. Can you even imagine doing this these days? It would take a day to fill all the policies and procedures out.

A few years later we got an updated vehicle that was red and had 'Excellence in Nursing Care' and our home's logo on the side. One of the resident's sons took thirteen of us to Manchester airport in May 1998 for us to jet off to Dublin for my fantastic hen weekend.

Most homes have brilliant slogans like ours. I have seen 'A Tradition of Excellence', 'A Legacy of Excellence', 'We are excellent' and 'Excellence is what we do'.

I've just actually made the last two up! They probably do exist somewhere in the world.

One of my favourite residents, Annie was so confused she did not know what day it was or whether it was winter or summer or day or night. One day a visitor came and said to me 'I think you should come into the lounge, Annie is causing havoc'. She was using the stacked music system as a walking aid and she was halfway across the room with all the wires hanging out of the wall. Maybe Kid Creole and the Coconuts were playing on the radio! Another time she got herself tangled up in the lining of the curtains. She will always bring a smile to my face every time I think of her. This lady was one of the most confused residents, but so lovely with it. She shocked me one day when she stopped with her zimmer frame and read from top to bottom every word of the fire escape rules on the wall. Then she was back to being extremely confused.

One cold winter's evening, my brother Joe and his friend Lee knocked on the kitchen window as Carole and I were in the kitchen scoffing a couple of left-over sandwiches. They had Annie with them. 'Is this one of your old biddies?' they asked. She had decided to go for an evening stroll. She had a handbag over each shoulder, criss-crossed over her chest, a blue hat and black gloves and her thick jam jar glasses. Carole and I brought her inside and thanked Joe and Lee very much for bringing her back. A keypad was installed on the front door the very next day.

I stamped on imaginary ants for one resident, told a ninety-three-year-old her mother would be back later, and told another lady in her eighties her babies were all settled and asleep. I did this out of empathy for the residents who suffered with dementia, as what they see or believe is so real and true to them. So I killed the imaginary ants on the bedroom floor, soothed the lady worrying about her mother and listened to how the other lady had run a nursery in her younger days. We cared a great deal about our residents.

One of Pam's favourite residents had a false eye, and would take it out at bedtime and place it in a tissue at the side of her bed. One morning the cleaners, Jan and Fran, had thrown it in the bin on their rounds. Panic set in so,

Pam reassured this resident that she would find it. So with my help we donned the plastic aprons and gloves and emptied all that morning's bin bags onto the back lawn and sieved through the masses of tissues. Old folks like tissues for some reason and tend to use loads and loads, but we had to open the scrunched-up tissues to look for the eye, so it was a yucky process. We were gipping and swearing until Pam screamed 'Yes, I've got it!' We danced around with such joy, as if we had found a diamond, but to this resident it was as precious as a diamond.

I was young and giddy when I started working there so and used to do silly things now and again. Tina, one of my colleagues, has recently reminded me of one such time. We were in the tiny lift, and I jumped up and down and it stopped. Tina went into a panic and the lovely lady from the kitchen had to wind it down and rescue us. I'm so sorry Tina, for making you scared of lifts.

A few of us had relatives working with us. Some of those who were mums were allowed to fetch their kids in for an hour if they were struggling after or before school time. It was such a happy, friendly place.

My sister Lucy worked part time in the kitchen loading and unloading the never-ending industrial dishwasher, and it felt like we were all one big family. Residents' family members liked us a lot and we formed some very good, trusting relationships.

Looking back, this is really the time in my career when

I laughed the most, because we had a smashing team and all of us had a great sense of humour. The home was well staffed. We used to play practical jokes on each other daily. Even though we were not making much money it didn't matter at that time. We loved going to work because we laughed such a lot. I will always be thankful and very proud to have experienced working in this nursing home with my brilliant friendly co-workers. My exceptional colleagues – my friends.

Coincidentally, years later I now live on the same street as the home, and I can see it from my bedroom window. My family gets sick of me saying 'oooh I worked hard in there,' every single time we walk past.

It's so sad that we now live in times of serious staffing shortages within the healthcare industry, with cutbacks, privatisation and more for less demanded of all employees. You only need to read a newspaper to see that stress and sickness in the workplace are at an all-time high. Staff are handing their notice in all the time, even staff members who have worked in the same place for many years. Experienced nurses are counting the days, months, even pay packets, down until they can retire. It is becoming a real crisis.

If I could afford not to work, I would, and I have wanted to retire since I turned forty. The people I have spoken to about retirement have different views about it. I am hoping this book becomes a best seller like that of

Adam Kay who is a well-known ex-doctor turned author. I expect most of my healthcare friends have read his books and watched 'This Is Going To Hurt', programme with him made by the BBC. My current role does not involve me doing a crazy number of steps per day any more or holding onto my bladder for longer than any human should, or not managing to eat on shift and getting lots of overtime. However, I did do all the above for a very long time.

Me in my ambulance uniform

With my friend Hazel

With Maggie, Carole and Pam

With Maggie at our graduation

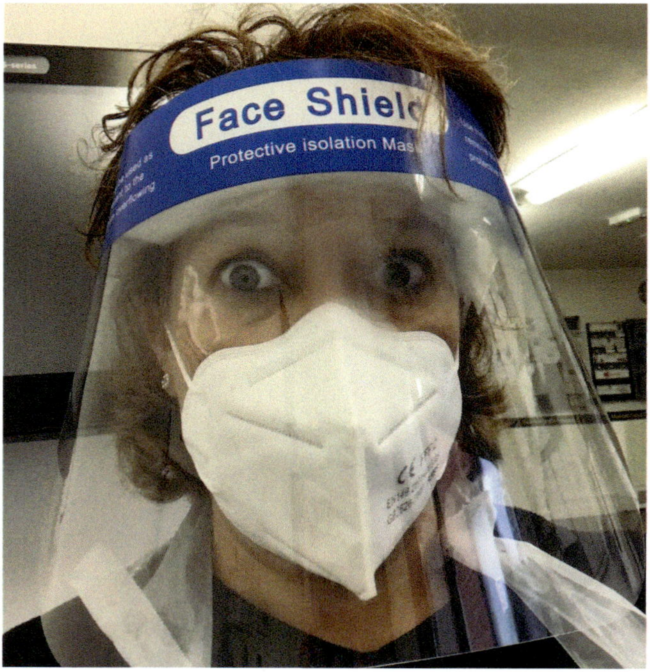

Me in my mask, working through Covid

Off to Dublin with my friends in the nursing home minibus, May 1998

Chapter 3

A change in career – becoming an agency HCA

Maggie had decided she wanted a change from working in the home and explained that she was going back into studying. Being the impulsive person I am, I replied, 'I'm coming with you'. I had done seven years at the nursing home and much as I loved it, I had decided I needed something else in my life at that time. Together we enrolled on a degree course. I would like to thank Maggie for letting me tag along and join her in going back into education. Plus, we did have a great time going to pubs – oh sorry, I mean being students and studying together! Our life's path takes us on many journeys and this one gave me another friend, Paul, who was one of my tutors. He and his wife Pauline have become good friends of ours. Paul read one of my first drafts of this book many years ago - thank you Paul.

Maggie and I both graduated in July 2000 with a degree

in social work and welfare studies. That was a very proud day for me. It was a huge achievement from the girl who just didn't grasp school.

Our studying was to last for four years. At the time I felt this was my ticket out of care work, but twenty years later my job title was still 'Health Care Assistant'. I might have been older and a tad wiser, but I was still doing the same job, the one I never thought I would go back to after completing my degree. More about this later.

Around the time when Maggie and I were enrolling on our course I was still working at the nursing home. One Saturday morning, we were short staffed, so an agency trained nurse came to help us. I recognised her as a former colleague from the first nursing home I had worked at and because I knew her, I was assigned to work alongside her. I explained to Taylar about the degree I was applying to do and said I was only really working when needed at the nursing home. Taylar explained to me that I would be better off working for the agency, mainly for the experience but also because the pay was much more than I was getting at the nursing home, which was not hard to believe! She wrote the agency's telephone number down on the back of my hand and told me to telephone them as soon as I got home.

I was quite dubious about ringing, although I was also thinking about the increase in wage I would receive if I got taken on. The pay is always a big issue with this type of work. It is disgustingly low for what is expected from you, and although thirty-plus years have passed it is still one of the lowest-paid jobs in healthcare. It's shocking that care work just isn't as recognised by many people, although year upon year thousands of cares are relied upon to support their nursing colleagues and do an incredible job. I know that all you nurses appreciate us, and we thank you.

Agency pay is very good in comparison to what nursing and residential homes and even the hospitals pay their own staff, so how could I not call them? I explained my commitments surrounding my degree course and was told this was not a problem. An interview was arranged for the following week. I was slightly nervous; on reflection this was because I had worked at the nursing home for seven years and regarded them as my work family. They had looked after me and taught me well, so I was a bit frightened and apprehensive about what might lie ahead in a new role.

I have moved around a few times in my career and was never afraid to do so again. It can make you feel and apprehensive, it may be a huge step to take, and sometimes it works out and sometimes it does not.

The fabulous job that was far from fabulous...

Here is an example of when it doesn't work out. After completion of my degree, I was so happy to get appointed for a company as Care Coordinator. I was given a different colour top to wear (navy) to differentiate me from the four staff I was to manage, who wore green tops. I was given a mobile phone, laptop and responsibilities. It was a brand-new venture, and I was appointed to help set up 'Crisis support' for a well-established company.

I worked my socks off for this company and lost weight through lack of sleep and stress. My confidence hit rock bottom, so I decided I needed to quit and went back to work in the field for the nursing agency.

I will just share with you one memory of my employment with this company. It was a horrendous home care shift with a tiny old lady who looked like she had been dragged through a hedge backwards. She had no children, just a nephew who lived in Scotland, and there was a photo of him on the fireplace. She had a care package in place with home care staff attending but she had got to the point of refusing any help or care.

This little old lady was unkempt and smelt quite bad. She was also vulnerable because her door was never locked due to the home care staff coming and going over the course of the day, so it was left on the latch to enable them to gain access.

I was called to provide a member of staff to spend the night with her when things had reached crisis point. There was nothing in her kitchen, no cups, plates, food or even tea bags for a drink. This was because she had meals on wheels brought in. There were no ornaments or knicknacks. just the photo of the nephew. I assumed that she just lived on the meals on wheels and had no treats or extras. I suppose with her not having any relations nearby treats and extras weren't being brought in. How sad, her home was such a mess. It was very demoralizing and depressing to see the state she and her home had got into. She was confused and kept looking at me and asking me why I was there and who had sent me. I tried to explain and be lovely and caring towards her, but she just kept giving me the evil eye.

I wasn't sodding well supposed to be there, but because my four people dressed in green polo shirts were being used elsewhere within the company, it unfortunately fell to me to attend.

I started at 8 pm, then at 9 pm in walked Gemma, who had arrived to do the nine-o clock slot. I knew Gemma from working with her in another place. She explained that this lady was extremely stubborn and had declined any help from the care staff. If they did try to give gentle persuasion, she lashed out at them, so they were coming in and not really doing anything for her. Gemma went on to explain that on many occasions they were coming in to find that she had been doubly incontinent and was sitting in it and had left a trail around her home, hence crisis point.

I excitedly explained to her that I had just spent the last four years studying to better myself. I caught her smirk and the look on her face told me what she was thinking. She might as well have said 'you wasted your time doing that then' as she wished me luck and skipped out of the door. It stung a bit as I sat down deflated and looked at the time; I had nine hours to go. I was already totally pissed off as this was not in my brilliant new job description.

I felt sick, as the aroma in this house was foul. I was hungry, tired and boiling hot due to the heating being on the highest setting possible, no brew all night just a can of Diet Coke and a Twix and wine gums to keep me going.

I tried my hardest to clean the mess up in her bedroom, but it had been there for some time so you can imagine the scene, and there was nothing to aid me. Just toilet roll there was, not even any wipes or gloves around. As always, I did have plastic gloves in my pocket. I learned early on to always have a pair in my pocket, but with no other aids to help me the gloves didn't really help in this instance.

Even though this was a long time ago and the lady will have passed away now, that night will be etched on my brain forever. I felt so sad for her she had dried poo on her body and didn't even realize it. As my dear Grandma used to say, 'there is no fun in getting old' and it is very true when the body starts to fail us.

That night made me question why I was doing the job, especially just after completion of four years of studying to better myself. After arguing with my boss about the twenty-four hours that I had just done, awake, she told me

I should have taken it as a sleep shift and carried on in the office the next day!

I thought, forget this, I'm going back to what I'm used to, and I could earn twice as much as they were paying me. I stood my ground and handed my notice in for the second and final time and off I went, back to the nursing agency.

When I saw the boss of that company years later, she apologised and said they had changed things after I had left, and she offered me my job back. I did think about it, but I declined her kind offer.

Paying for your health care, and us working free hours

On quite a few shifts, especially at one of the private hospitals I worked in, I would often not get off on time, this has a knock-on effect because you are then hurrying to get home in the morning rush hour traffic to enable your husband to get off to work or to get the children sorted.

Here is an example. We had had a busy night shift and by 6 am we had that exhausted feeling. There were three of us, me and two trained staff. One of them was doing the medication round and I was giving a bed bath to a lady who had had surgery the previous day,so she had a drip and a PCA machine attached (Patient Controlled Analgesia). This task needed two staff, but I could start collecting all the items we would need and then start the bed bath and tidying the room whilst my colleague finished off whatever she was attending to.

I had done what I could on my own, so I went to find my colleague to say I was ready for her help. She had been held up by another patient who had had the runs and had not reached the loo in time. So, as you can imagine the little task that she was doing changed into a time-consuming one. Many healthcare jobs do that. I wanted to help her, but I had also left a patient half bed bathed so I needed to get back to her to explain, but you can't say 'My colleague is busy cleaning poo up'. You just have to say they have got held up. This lady was half done and I couldn't do any more until I had another pair of hands to help me. She explained that she was experiencing a lot of pain, so I decided to go and find my other colleague who was still doing the medication round. I explained that my patient had pain and needed some medication and the nurse said she was on her way. If we just had another staff member to help us it would have made all the difference.

I went back to the patient to explain, and she looked upset and was saying she had a LOT of pain. I felt hopeless because there was nothing I could do to help. I didn't want to leave her on her own, but I also didn't want to be in this awkward position. The patient then started to cry, and I felt so bad for her and really wanted someone else to come in the room to help me. I had already explained the situation to both of my colleagues so they both knew they were needed in this room but were doing other important tasks. I reassured this lady as much as I could and advised her that I would go and find some help. The day staff had now arrived, so I explained the situation to the day Sister and was told they would just have the handover and then they would be in to take over.

I went back to the patient and felt terrible that all I seemed to keep doing was making excuses for no one coming, she was a private paying patient and this always makes matters worse – I know it shouldn't, but it does. Ask yourself this question: if you were paying for medical care, would you have been disappointed with that? I think I would have been a tiny bit peed off.

She was still very upset and taking deep breaths for her pain and all I could do was pass her a tissue for the tears and be there, even though I really didn't want to be there at that moment. Then, after which seemed like ages, the day staff came in for their handover from the night sister. I was supposed to end my shift at eight, but how could I say that to her when there was no one else to help and she was obviously in pain? I couldn't leave her until she had been handed over to the day staff. I kept glancing at the clock. She knew it was the end of my shift and she kept telling me to go, but I reassured her that I would not leave her until someone else arrived. I think she settled slightly knowing this and was thanking me and she seemed a little calmer.

As she was settling, I was stressing. I knew I should

have been well on my way home by now. I was conscious of the time, and it was a school day. I was also aware that it had been a frosty night and I had no de-icer.

The day staff took over and said I could leave. I apologised yet again to the patient and eventually got out at half past eight. The computer we use to fill in our timesheets was now being used by the ward clerk and because I wasn't permanent staff, stupidly I didn't ask to ask to change it. Looking back, throughout my agency shifts there were probably loads of hours when I worked for free. I know I am not alone in that. I know that all of us who work under the umbrella of healthcare put in unpaid hours, miss breaks and rarely leave on time. The medical industry gets thousands of free hours from their dedicated staff – I wonder how many politicians work for free. I want to mention the admin and medical secretaries, as they also often stay behind to send urgent emails, mainly to the coroner's office. Ask any admin staff and they will tell you that an urgent email or request from the qualified staff will more often than not come through just as they are getting ready to leave the office.

It always has a knock-on effect when you can't get off on time, and it happens a lot in this profession.

Rudeness

During my time as an HCA, I cared for some of the

most obnoxious, rude and miserable people. We are all individuals at any age, some nice, but some not so nice.

To be honest there were more sweet, nice people than rude ones. When you're an agency employee some residents can make you feel unwelcome by saying things sarcastically whilst looking you up and down. 'Oh, now then we haven't seen you before, I bet you don't know where such and such is' and tut-tut if you don't position their tissue box in the exact spot where they like it.

I had just done a night shift in one of the private hospitals and I was emptying a catheter (urine) bag and as usual, being me a chatterbox, I was making polite conversation. The patient was asking far too many questions about other patients; he was wanting to know details which I wasn't prepared to tell him. He said to me 'too hard a question?' and I replied 'I don't know'. I had been awake for a lot of hours and was knackered. I thought right, you cheeky sod, so I gave him a right good spiel about confidentiality and how I would not dream of telling any of our other patients any details about him, and that was why I had replied that I didn't know, not because it was a hard question to answer – I wasn't thick. He did apologise to me but did not get the bed bath I was going to offer. However, he did get the V sign with both hands as I left his room. I did the Vs quite often when I was an HCA to some bossy staff members and patients, it made me feel better. I still do it to this day, mainly to my two teenagers!

I wonder if he would have said that to a trained member of staff. He had probably driven a shiny status symbol car with a personalised plate, maybe with a set of golf clubs in the boot. He looked that type. As Basil Fawlty put it, 'You snobs'.

The agency and my new role within it

I started work for a well-established nursing agency from 1998, when I was twenty-six . I had ten years' experience under my belt as a carer, so I was ready for a change, and my new role began as a part-time office coordinator. This was something I took to straight away and I knew I was going to enjoy my new position; I thrived in the busy office and met many wonderful staff, and two great colleagues, Jean & Veronica. Sadly, Jean passed away at the young age of 57 years. RIP my friend.

I did keep my hand in as an HCA, and I picked up the occasional bank holiday shifts and a few Friday night shifts, where you could earn good money.

Then two kids, arrived in our lives. After number two child came along, I had to give up my office hours to care for two babies, so I decided to go back as an HCA 'out in the field'. The hours fitted into our family life better than the office hours, so I did what a lot of mums do, working the hours and jobs that fitted in with babies and children. I said goodbye to the agency office in 2006.

Working in so many medical establishments, I quickly had to grow an overcoat of thick skin. I stopped letting people upset me as I had done in the beginning with the little snippets of bitchiness and snide comments about how agency staff get more money. That was the biggest bone of contention and probably still is to this day. I learned very quickly to take all the disparaging comments on the chin, and it is good not getting involved with their politics, gossip and problems that most establishments have. The flip side is not being part of a team, any team, not being invited on nights outs, Christmas parties and not forming good working relationships with colleagues.

Some people say if you're doing the same job, you should get paid the same. I don't agree with this and never will. If you work hard and are a team player and have more years' experience than another colleague, what incentive is there to carry on being all those things if you get the same pay as an inexperienced, lazy person? And believe me when I say I have worked with some idle co-workers over the years.

As agency, bank and locum staff do not get as many contractual entitlements as permanent employed staff receive, there must be an incentive to do it, and that's the amount of pay. There were a few times when I did not get a call for a shift when I had indicated my availability, but this thankfully didn't happen often. Of course it's a bit scary when you have children to clothe and feed and bills to pay.

Some situations I found myself in whilst working for the agency are hard to believe. On many occasions I felt disliked just for being an agency employee. I collected many articles about agency staff for this book, but found that every one of them I read was the same. One argument is that it is all about poor planning and how disgusting it is that agency bosses can make a profit from the NHS. However, the reality is that the healthcare industry simply could not function without agency staff.

The tabloids blame agency staff for the huge bills charged to health authorities with many headlines reading something like this '*Fears over the cost of hospital relief workers*' and '*Nursing tycoon gets* £3m from *NHS*'. There will always be articles in magazines and newspapers regarding the cost of relief staff and how it is a massive drain on the industry. Here are two quotes from my local newspaper: '*Staff are already working under a lot of pressure. Having to work alongside someone you might have to mentor because they are not used to the working environment only adds to this pressure*'.

I totally agree with this statement. But another article said: '*The use of agency and hospital bank staff is essential to help the trust deal with additional pressures*'. I also totally agree with this statement, but what is the answer?

I always found that others who had also worked for an agency had more tolerance of me, perhaps a little hint of a bond, camaraderie even. Looking back now, I really do not know how I did it for all those years.

Whilst I worked within the agency office, I found that many staff could only stick at it for a short spell of time. When we took on a new member of staff and they knew I also worked out in the field I felt they had more respect for me, as they knew that I knew exactly what they were going through. We had staff ringing us up in tears saying they had just been spoken to like shit and they didn't want to go back in after their breaks. One highly strung nurse rang us to say she had done a full circle of the huge hospital car park and there was not one free space. We had to use all our persuasive skills to keep her there whilst the head of the bank staff went out in the rain and managed to get her a space. She was ready to speed off home.

On a lot of occasions, I had to hold back my tears and was treat terribly by other staff members, as the stranger. It is difficult to work with someone you don't know. They don't know anything about you and vice versa, and you get paired up on a shift. It is no wonder the regular staff get fed up when they are the chosen one to work alongside the agency stranger. They would much rather be with their colleagues, people they have got to know and maybe have a friendship with.

A friend of mine was having a good old moan about how much harder her job becomes when they start to bring in a lot of agency staff. She worked alongside a very young HCA who in her words was a lazy sod. She explained that she had left the room to collect something and on return he was just sitting on the patient's bed. She said, 'Why don't you make that bed instead of sitting on it?' but she felt quite mean saying it, because she had herself worked for an agency for a time and knew how hard it can be. We both came to the conclusion that whoever it is, agency or not, if someone is being a lazy sod then they should be told. I know some agency staff *are* lazy and they feel they can get away with acting as if they don't know what to do or where anything is.

I really do understand the frustrations of the permanent staff's attitude towards agency staff because I have worked alongside some of the lazy ones who do not have any experience or appreciate what is needed to succeed. I have also worked with excellent agency staff who had common sense, a thick skin and just got on with it, as I did. And they definitely do not sit on a bed when it needs making!

I think the main reason for most of the permanent staff's dislike of agency staff is the lack of experience, whether of the actual job or the patients and the building. It just makes a short staffing problem much worse. If the permanent staff weren't fed up enough, they know that this stranger, good or bad, is getting paid significantly more money than them.

When I was employed by the nursing home they were always asking us to fill extra shifts and I always said I would do it for fifty pence an hour extra. Of course this was never allowed, but what I couldn't get my head round was they would employ agency staff and give them more than it would have cost to give me the extra fifty pence I asked for.

When I joined a shift for the first time and entered a room full of staff with all eyes upon me, I was asked, 'Have you been here before?' I used to cringe if I had to say no because they would openly roll their eyes, and some hard-faced ones would tut-tut. Carole told me a story of a time when she arrived on a ward at one of the big NHS hospitals ready to work her shift and not one of the regular staff welcomed or spoke to her on arrival after she had explained that she was from the nursing agency. She decided to stand and wait until someone did. After some time the sister in charge asked her if she was ok and Carole explained that she had introduced herself at the nursing station on arrival and was ignored, so she was happy to wait as she was getting paid and if her staff didn't want her help she would just wait. Sister was not pleased and assigned her to work alongside a staff member. Again, I think all of us relief staff have been in situations like this. Now you can understand where your thick skin comes in handy if you're relief staff.

I got to the stage of just saying 'yes, I have been here before'. They don't give you anything to help you help them – for example, a list of room numbers and names would be a huge bonus.

In my experience of the first time in a new place, you are totally thrown in at the deep end. They should show you round and point out helpful things like how to cancel a buzzer, fire exits, toilets, just to name a few. But they are far too busy for that and too short staffed. Also the staff are miffed because we are getting more wages than them, so why should they go out of their way to help us? Because you haven't been shown these things you make mistakes. For example, the first time you go to answer a buzzer there are many different kinds, and if you get one you're not familiar with, you end up setting the emergency buzzer off and stand there thinking shit, shit, shit as all the other staff come running to help. Someone sorts it out and you can see what they are thinking and will say about you out of earshot, but you were only trying to help.

I think that every establishment should give relief staff a list of residents' names, room numbers and which floor they are on, or even a map of the building like the ones you get at the theme parks just to pop in their pocket for the duration of the shift. A brief description of how to cancel a buzzer and how to activate the emergency buzzer would be very beneficial. I know we get a handover but if you have never been in a place before, and some places are massive, I really think this would help.

Also, from experience of being given the job of taking the tea trolley round on several occasions, a drink list would be helpful. In all the places I worked at only one residential home one of my favourite places to work did this, and it was a huge help.

Talking of tea trolleys, it always used to make me laugh how some trained staff had an allergic reaction to them. One nurse in particular who used to work in the nursing home with us used to say to everyone 'I did not do my nurse training to push a tea trolley around'. Yeah, fair comment, but she would take a brew and biscuits from it and go and sit on her lazy arse whilst buzzers were going off.

When I worked in the nursing home, I did like to take the tea trolley round in the afternoon, as I love a biscuit and helped myself to quite a few. I liked to see every resident and their relations and I always used to say 'you're sweet enough' if they didn't take sugar in their drink. I always got a smile or a laugh when I said it.

Chapter 4

It takes all sorts...

Different types of staff

Because I have worked with so many different kinds of staff over the years, I have formed my own definitions. If you're a care worker, I will let you choose which one suits you the best.

Young – Usually found in rest or nursing homes; some are there to gain experience for the road into nurse training. Some, like me, will do the job for ten years plus and be content to gain experience and qualifications, becoming happy working as an HCA.

It would be unfair to tar all young carers with the same brush because I have worked with some lovely ones. I started in this job very young myself, and I know I was a pain sometimes and could be childish, because I didn't have the life experience that I have now.

I remember working with one girl who was very young

and inexperienced – I'll call her Meredith. It was a night shift in a large rest home, and I was biting my tongue most of the night because she seemed much too immature and cocky to be there. She was new and had only been there two weeks, and I felt she was showing off in front of me.

A resident followed this girl into the kitchen and was asking for her usual bedtime drink. Meredith turned to her and said, 'can you get out of here, you're not allowed to be in here' and then turned to me and said, 'don't they know how to wind you up'. I put my arm round the frail old lady's shoulders and asked her to show me to her room, saying I would bring the drink to her in two ticks. I was biting hard on my lip. Later she went on to admit, laughing and without shame, that she had been suspended from her last job because she had written on a care plan 'still dead' when a resident had passed away! I did not bite my lip this time – I tried to explain in a nice way why we don't say and do such things. I bet she thought I was a condescending cow.

Plodders – Most of these carers are found in rest or nursing homes, but many work in the hospitals. They do not want to venture away from their comfort zone. They are quite happy just to do their elected hours, though they can sometimes can be coaxed into doing the odd extra if really persuaded, but will let everyone around them know about it.

They are adamant that they do not want to study for

any qualifications and say 'I'm not studying, what do I want that for, been doing this job x years, what can they teach me that I don't already know? No, I'm not doing it'. Don't get me wrong - the have buckets full of experience and there isn't much they don't know about the job, so student nurses learn a great deal from them.

Home carers – These are rushed people, always hurrying around trying to find extra hours within their working day. They always look stressed and often smoke a lot. Sorry, I know some of you are not stressed and don't smoke either!

I did do a few home care shifts, and found these shifts much more personal and lonely than working in an establishment. You are entering personal space and are placed in a position of great trust. I was asked to do a few nights with a lady whose health had declined rapidly, and the family were paying for extra help. I got close to her and her daughter and I was upset when she passed away. I will always remember these shifts as it was the time when Madeline McCann went missing in 2007 and I was watching the harrowing story on news all night.

I couldn't switch off the same way when I left her because sometimes she was alone and was very poorly when it was my time to leave, so I was staying over my allotted time, and I found that aspect of the job hard. I wanted to get home to see my children, but felt so dreadful to be leaving her alone until her daughter could get to her.

Thankfully there are staff that love being a home care HCA and they provide a vital role in helping the elderly to stay in their own homes, which is what they all want to do if possible, so again thank goodness there are lots of brilliant home carers.

There are also MCAs, Maternity Care Assistants, who are very experienced and assist in the resuscitation of newborns, although I have not worked in that department. I also know a good few GP practice HCAs, and again they are worth their weight in gold as they do so much to assist in the running of a practice, minor ops, anticoagulant and diabetic clinics just to name a few – I myself have stepped in as a Practice HCA on a few occasions to assist in the minor op and coil clinics. I felt like I was a very important person passing the implements to the doctor.

My seven types of nurse

Hard and a bit scary – This nurse tends to be a textbook of information and has vast experience. Tells it like it is, swears a lot and does not care who is listening whilst offloading about colleagues, patients, doctors or whoever else has pissed them off. Speaks about things they have done in the good old days without shame and just as you are asking yourself why they are in the caring profession you catch them with a patient and see or hear something that proves they are amazingly experienced and amazingly caring. We need nurses like this for various uniquely tough roles.

Leading – Won't stand no messing, no mollycoddling, tells it exactly as it is, and speaks clearly and concisely with their instructions. Extremely well organised, exceptionally thorough, neat and tidy, never forgets anything needed to carry out their job. When they are in charge everything is done to a good standard and the shift seems calm. Can get frustrated when colleagues don't work the same way and often find it hard to switch off, so they take work home with them.

Soft and 'faffy' – treats every patient with empathy, respect, dignity, and privacy and has the patience of a saint. Has shed a tear or two whilst on duty, and faffs about doing things that could be left till it's less busy. Lots of this type of nurses leave the profession because they can't hack it.

Brilliant – very experienced but has not let all that experience turn into arrogance, never speaks out of turn about a patient on handover, very professional and caring, rolls their sleeves up and gets stuck in, and never ever forgets to say thank you to the HCAs they work with. Shelagh you are under this one, and Belinda, as you always thanked me on our shifts together.

Be right – Sticks to what needs doing and not much more and says things like 'it will do' and 'is it nearly time to go home yet?' quite chilled out, knows what to do in a crisis, sorts it then has a brew, biscuit, fag, and another break. My previous colleagues from the second nursing home will know exactly who I have modelled this one on!

RMN (Registered Mental Health Nurse) – RMNs come under a category all on their own and are amazing and calm.

Nursing staff from prison / psychiatric / paediatric/ hospice/ general practice / midwife / health visitor and every single healthcare worker on this earth are all, in my eyes, amazing and super humans.

There are also still a few dual registered nurses out there – this means they have trained to work as a mental health nurse and also a general nurse. They are worth a million dollars and have a huge fount of knowledge, and they are like gold dust these days.

There was an amazing one I worked a lot with on my agency shifts – Fred. I always felt so much better when I knew he was my colleague on shift, because I had huge respect for him. He was so knowledgeable about nursing, and we shared a rude sense of humour. I learnt recently that he had passed away. RIP Fred.

Chapter 5

Some shifts to remember

My first agency shift

My first shift was in June 1998. It was a night shift, in a nursing home not too far from where I lived at the time. A friend of mine from the home where I used to work had told me that one of our residents had gone to this nursing home because she had become very aggressive. She had lashed out at one of the other residents and there had been a complaint, so she had to be moved. This lady, Mrs V, had been one of my favourites, so I was looking forward to seeing her. I don't care what anyone says, you always have your favourites as with people generally, you gel with some better than others.

It was a Friday night, and I was a bit anxious driving to this home. I knew I could do the job – it was the staff I would be working with that I was worrying about. I had only ever done one night shift in all the years I had worked at the nursing home. I was to start at ten and work till 8 am. I made sure I arrived in plenty of time, and I explained who I was to the nurse who was overseeing the evening shift. The smell of wee hit me as soon as I walked through the door.

The trained nurse took me along to the staff room, which of course back then was always a fag smoke-filled room with half-empty bottles of pop, cardigans, full ashtrays, half-dead looking plants, umbrellas, mugs with names on lying around. Always a sign above the sink saying something like 'if you use it wash it' or 'do not leave dirty pots in this sink'.

There were three to four girls in the room, and no one really spoke to me. I was ignored quite a lot during my time on the agency, because I was just not part of the team, the clique.

Thankfully one of the girls asked me my name and this broke the ice. I explained that I used to look after Mrs V and asked how she was doing. One of the girls said that she would take me to see her later. Then at about five to ten some of the staff were ready to leave and the girl who had asked my name took me along to the office for handover, or report as some people call it. All caring establishments do this as it is important for the staff coming on to know what changes have taken place. So much can happen in a single shift whether it's morning, evening or the night shift.

The evening nurse told me that the trained nurse for our

shift was coming from the same agency as myself. I then saw a car pull into the car park and recognised it as Graham's. I had worked with him previously and I think he got a shock when he saw me standing there ready for a night shift. He is a very clever man with many qualifications, and highly professional. I was relieved to be working with him. Once the handover had been given to us, and all the evening staff had left, it was our turn to work. There were four of us for about thirty residents.

On a night shift, whether in a hospital or a care home, it's important to do what is called a 'back round', ie go round the establishment and do a check on all the residents, changing them if they have been incontinent and make them comfortable. Turning or adjusting their position is another crucial requirement as this prevents pressure sores.

Residents in homes can be there for many reasons. Often the family cannot commit to the twenty-four-hour care that is needed to look after a loved one, plus there is the financial element to consider. Their loved one may be confused, elderly and frail, and often doubly incontinent.

Most homes have a trolley that is stocked up with the things you will need: bed linen, incontinence products, towels, plastic gloves and wipes. Sadly some places I attended were not as well stocked up as others. This used to annoy me as these things are needed for us to be able to give basic care.

On doing a back round staff also check that the

resident is clean, comfortable and free of any pain. This in most homes and hospitals is done every two hours through the night. Often a resident will need their incontinence pad changing and sometimes their bedclothes and bed sheets will need a full change. Although this task is a time-consuming one, my opinion is that once you have washed, changed and made the resident dry and comfortable you can see in their faces that they feel better, clean and comfortable again, even though you might have to do the same thing all over again with the same resident in two hours' time.

On this night we split up and worked in pairs. Graham went with one of the girls, Hannah, and I with the other, Katie. They explained that two would work on one side of the building and the other two on the other side. Katie took me along to our side and we did a back round and checked on all the residents. We also put a gentleman into bed and made him comfortable. We then went along to see Mrs V. She looked so different. She had lost a lot of weight and was deteriorating, which was sad to see. She was awake, so I said hello to her and wondered if she remembered me. I was probably just another face to her. I like to think that she did remember me, although she had got so confused she wouldn't know if it was Florence Nightingale who was checking her incontinence pad. I gave her a little kiss on the head and said hi, and I managed to get a smile out of her.

We met up with the other two and Hannah suggested a brew. I was so hot and thirsty I could have drunk ten cups of tea. I was so relieved to have a break.

We went along to the messy staff room, all taking a turn to walk the building to check all was calm. We stayed there until it was time to do the next back round. We had to change almost all our residents. We also found a lady wandering about the corridor, so we put her back to bed and made her comfortable. I also found another lady wandering around like a zombie and this poor lady was stark naked. Luckily she was leaning on the trolly, so I grabbed a sheet and wrapped her up, then took her to find Katie to advise me to which number this lady's bedroom was. There were so many the obstacles and various other hurdles I found myself facing on almost every shift.

Once we had finished the round we went into the laundry and put all the wet sheets into the washing machine. I could not believe my eyes when I walked into the laundry – it was so untidy and there were clothes all over in great big piles. Katie asked me if I would mind going round all the residents' rooms that we had just been into and check what clothes were needed for the morning. She told me to get a clean incontinence pad and write down the room number and what items of clothing were needed onto the pad. I did as asked, thinking this was a bit strange.

I went into the first room and looked in the drawers and wrote on the pad what was required for the morning. I thought it was so sad that the residents had nothing in their drawers and their clothes were all in that untidy laundry. It was even sadder when a resident was awake in bed just staring at me, me a stranger looking in her cupboards and drawers. I remember feeling sorrowful for this resident, two strangers in the dead of night just looking at each other in a very dimly lit room smelling of wee, with not much furniture in it, just a few reminders of a past life – photos and trinkets on the top of the drawers and me standing there looking at her in bed. I just smiled lovingly at her, thinking of my own grandparents.

This task was very time consuming, and I reported back to Katie in the laundry with all the pads that I had written on. She explained that their approach was to find the items that were required and then roll them up inside the pad and put them all back into the residents' rooms. Some residents only needed knickers, and some needed everything: knickers, underpants, underskirts, stockings and vests. Katie got hold of a pad and read what I had written. She did not look to see if the knickers were for the right person, she just went through a gigantic pile of clean washing for the items she needed, regardless of what size and who the items belonged to.

I really could not get over this, so I asked why the laundry was in such a state and she replied that it was because of the residents being elderly mentally infirm (EMI) cases. They were all very incontinent, and the laundry girl could simply not catch up with all the washing. I found myself comparing the laundry with the nursing home where I used to work and there was just no comparison – this one was in a terrible mess. I felt that I wanted to spend a day sorting through it all to sort out who the clothes belonged to who and put them all back into their rooms, but sadly most of the items did not have name tags on and the ones that did were unreadable as they had been washed so many times. So, we just completed the 'pad task' and put them in the appropriate rooms for the morning. This was a very long time ago; I hope they have a much better system in place nowadays. However, if I had gone to help, I might have turned everything pink! I also went into a panic about myself getting old and being put in some other person's knickers. I hope I would be so confused that I wouldn't notice.

We then had another break. We did not sit in the messy smoky staff room, this time we placed folded sheets onto the comfortable chairs in the day room and sat in there and watched television. The reason we placed the sheets on the chairs was because incontinent residents had been sitting on the chairs during the day. Many times, I went home with smelly wee on my pants where I had sat down on a wet chair or knelt onto the floor in a patch of wee.

As we sat watching telly there was a resident shouting out gibberish. She was getting louder and louder, so I went to look and see if she was ok, Hannah and Katie explained that she did this most nights. She would wake one or two others up and they would also start shouting gibberish very loudly or banging relentlessly. When a confused resident starts shouting it is mainly repetitive words that do not make any sense and they go on and on and on. There is nothing you can do to stop them, apart from give them medicine, mainly tranquillisers, but in a lot of cases the medicine does not seem to touch them.

I spent a bit of time with this woman, who was happily confused. I had a little chat to her, and she seemed to like me. We chatted about all sorts of stuff and had a bit of a laugh; it was like talking to a happy drunk. I returned to the lounge when she seemed settled, feeling quite proud of myself, but then ten minutes later, she was shouting again.

We completed another few back rounds – they should name them backbreaking rounds, with all the bending and lifting we do. Katie and I found a resident had had a poo in the sink in his room, so we dealt with that little mishap, thankfully he had not made too much mess, he just thought the sink was the toilet. At least he didn't wipe his bum on the curtains.

We did our best in the laundry throughout the night, then at 6 am we started getting the residents up for the day. We washed and dressed, lifting and bending, let me tell you it really was absolutely backbreaking. Most of the residents could not take their own weight. Some even lifted their feet off the ground, so we were actually physically lifting then up by their arms, which key lifters will find horrifying (key lifters are appointed in most caring establishments to teach moving and handling techniques). I like to think that this probably doesn't happen quite as much any more because health and safety has come to the forefront in the workplace and people do think about it now, but in 1998, we just lifted. One, two, three lift.

It is now an annual requirement that moving and handling techniques are taught throughout the healthcare industry at a high standard and staff must use hoists, slide sheets and lots of aids to help when the patient is non-weight-bearing. I did used to find that in larger homes the carers found using the hoist very time consuming, so physical lifting was quicker. I did see a hoist, in the back of a cupboard with blankets strewn over it. I felt very nauseous, and my head was booming at eight am with the dehydration, humidity, hunger and tiredness. I was so relieved that it was time to go home. There could not have been many residents left in their beds because between the four of us we had got almost all of them up, washed and dressed.

I got home and put my wee pants on a hot wash, had some toast plus a lovely shower and collapsed into bed. I don't know how I survived on night shifts – they are killers.

That was my first ever agency shift, and I was never asked to work there again. Maybe they sorted their staffing problems out or maybe other agency staff covered the shifts; I don't suppose I will ever know. I wonder if the pad task is still used. I really hope not.

I do know Hannah and Katie were nice girls to work with and they lulled me into thinking everyone else would be like this!

I will always remember that first shift.

My last-ever agency shift – A&E department

Even though I now had years of experience under my belt, I must admit I was still quite apprehensive about my first shift in an A&E department. Would it be like Casualty, Holby City or Grey's Anatomy? The Sister in charge seemed quite hostile towards everyone in the staff room prior to the shift starting. I had a bad gut feeling about this shift. There were many staff ready to go on duty and just one of them spoke to me. It turned out that her daughter, whom I knew, also worked as an HCA for the same agency as myself.

Sister allocated everyone their positions for the night. I wasn't allocated anywhere, so I just followed them out of the office onto the department like a lamb to the slaughter.

Everyone scattered like confetti in the wind. There were phones ringing, doctors and medical staff all over the place, ambulance crew bringing patients in on trolleys to the side entrance. It was sheer bedlam, and it wasn't even a weekend.

Two police officers arrived with an extremely intoxicated patient and asked me which cubical to put him in. I looked around, and luckily for me a charge nurse took over and I just followed, feeling incompetent. One of the police officers asked me another question to which I didn't really know the answer, so I just explained that I was an agency worker who had not been on this department before. Mr policeman was really nice and handsome, and he gave me a wink and lovely smile before leaving us with the drunken man. I remember feeling so useless and just wanting not to be there, plus it didn't help as the charge nurse turned to me and said, 'I'm ok in here thanks' . He might as well have said 'I don't want you in here helping me so sod off'.

As I left that room a patient's relative asked me where the nearest toilet was and I had to explain again that I was new and had not been shown myself. We decided that it couldn't be too far away and that we would find it together. Another useless moment and only an hour had passed. Sister arrived and asked me to transfer a patient from the A&E ward to the gynaecology ward, then come back to work on the A&E ward. I got back down from escorting the gynae patient and went round the corner onto the ward, where I met by a not very happy HCA. He was a massive drama queen voicing his feelings about being swapped with me, and his nurse colleague looked as joyous as he did. He did not introduce himself or his colleague, just expressed his frustrations at having to swap around and work where he clearly did not want to. He was voicing his frustrations regarding agency staff as if I was invisible. He then had the decency to say, 'no offence'. All I wanted to do was say 'Right, fuck you lot I'm off home,' but much as I really wanted to, I did not.

I walked up and down the small ward and a patient beckoned for me and asked me to pass him his Fibogel from his cabinet, so I did; it's an over-the-counter medicine that helps with constipation. Not long after this, the drama queen came over and explained that I was to go back round to the department and he was staying on *his* ward, so off I went round the corner.

I went to see if the nurse in resuscitation needed any assistance. She was looking after two patients who were poorly but stable, and she seemed nice and said I could stay and assist. I relaxed. I must have let my guard down because I began to moan about feeling useless, and how I wanted to go and work on one of the other wards that I was more used to.

My next task was to escort a patient to X-ray. On return I felt that maybe the nurse from resuscitation might have had a word with Sister, because she came over to me and apologised that no one had shown me round. However, she then went on to say that it was pointless sending relief staff to A & E because it was such a specialist department. Obviously, someone had asked for this shift to be filled by agency staff!

She asked me what I was used to doing and started to show me round but was then needed so had to dash off. I spotted the other HCA working on the department and asked her if I she needed any help. She asked me to take some observations from a patient who also proceeded to ask me loads of questions that I did not have answers to.

Sister then came to me and asked if she could have a word. She said 'I don't know what you are allowed to do at your other hospital [I also banked at another hospital and had told her this], but here we don't let HCAs, especially agency HCAs, give drugs out'. I quickly worked out that she must have been talking about the Fibogel, because that was all I could relate it to.

She explained that she would have to ring the agency and fill in an incident form. I could have kicked myself. I uttered an apology, and she scurried off. This didn't help my already low self-esteem level, and when I saw a baby being brought in clinging to its mother, I had to use all my power to stop the tears from flowing, because I wanted to go home to my own babies.

A staff nurse must have sensed my upset and said I could shadow her. She was nice and made me feel a lot better. I assisted her with the clean-up of a gentleman who had fallen and cut his face quite badly, but was in good spirits considering his injuries. We then went round to cover on the A&E ward whilst the drama queen and his mate, who never once made eye contact or spoke to me, went on their breaks. I stayed with this nice nurse until her shift ended at midnight. Things seemed to have calmed down by the early hours and some of us had a brew together. At one point I had a chance to chat with Sister and found she was not hostile at all, she was just a very well-experienced, well-trained and focused A&E nurse.

The first thing I did when my shift ended at 07.45 was to contact my boss at the Agency and warn her that she might get a call about the Fibogel incident (thankfully she never did). I still believe the drama queen grassed on me!

I also explained that I had just worked my last shift. All the crap shifts, upset, tears and hours spent traveling, no workmates and endless painstaking graft were over. Finally, my time as an Agency Health Care Assistant had ended, and that A&E shift helped me make up my mind. I felt free.

My penultimate shift for the agency was also a tough one, as you will hear next.

I can't really tell you the main reason for my decision to give up. I possibly could have carried on longer if the wages had been brilliant. I only brought home £59.58 for this ten-hour A&E shift, but somewhere along the way I had changed and realised that as agency staff you are never, ever part of a team, and an agency career is a long time to be the outsider.

Anyway, back to the story.

Penultimate shift - Auld Lang Syne

All I can say when I reflect on this shift is 'OMG!' I most definitely earned my wage. Like the Proclaimers, I walked five hundred miles that particular New Year's Eve.

Anyone who has ever set foot or worked, or is still working, in a Medical Assessment Unit (MAU) will know how extremely busy they are, day and night. This one was large, so the staff were split into three teams. I was given a handover for team two, but because the ward was so busy, I was all over the place and answering buzzers for the other teams. I did not know the names of patients because I hadn't had handover for team one and I hadn't got the foggiest what was wrong with them.

Other wards I had worked on had patient names above their beds and that helps, but this one just had numbers. Sometimes their notes or observation sheets were next to them, but not often.

This ward, being a large one, was always so busy. There were cups and half-empty bottles everywhere and bits of rubbish all over, so I got a trolley and collected all the pots, cans, and bottles and did a general tidy-up. It's amazing how just a little tidying can make such a difference. Sister thanked me for doing it.

I could have done with some spray to wipe all the patients' tables down but couldn't find any. As I was tidying up, I went into a day room and an elderly lady said

'Oh thank goodness you have come, I've been here ages'. I went to fetch Sister and she was told she could go. From the look of things I think she had been forgotten about, but I could be wrong.

The ward seemed so untidy. For example, bedding was just left on the side in one bay, bits of dressings were left all over the place on tables, and the floor was littered with all sorts of things.

On such a busy ward as this staff must act fast. You are so busy there just isn't the time to tidy up after yourself. Maybe a visitor or someone with no understanding of how fast you have got to work would look at this and think 'what a mess!'

I can relate this to another shift I worked in another location where one patient had extremely low blood pressure, so the RMO (Resident Medical Officer) wanted me to check it again for him. A patient was buzzing because she wanted her dressing changed, the front door bell was going, the telephone was ringing, my one and only colleague Shelagh was in another room doing an ECG, and a patient's relative was waiting for a coffee to be made for him. There were just the two of us and I certainly wasn't too bothered about cleaning my mess up after me. In situations like that it's the least of your worries. I did clean and tidy up after myself on this shift, as I had the time to do it before my shift ended. However, in A&E and specialized wards and departments, all the staff are constantly working nonstop and never get a quiet period to tidy up. Never mind a quick brew or loo break, they work non-stop until it's their thirty-minute break time. Many nurses, mainly in the higher bands, eat at a computer as there just isn't enough time to have a break. In a lot of healthcare establishments there are always staff shortfalls, so it falls to line managers to complete the work whilst on their lunch breaks.

Again, I know I keep saying this, but it needs repeating. Overstretched, unappreciated and underfunded. I know all of you who work in the medical profession reading this will relate.

That night I must have gone on escort with half of the patients and the same porter about ten times all the way down to x-ray or on to other wards. After all these trips up and down and left and right, Mr Porter and I had time to have a good chat with each other. He was a great bloke, and we had a laugh. Porters do not get a good enough wage for what they do. It's wrong and it's time pay scales in healthcare roles were changed.

I just got back onto the ward to watch the fireworks going off at midnight. All the lights were dimmed down, and it was a brilliant view as the ward was on the fourth or fifth floor. I shed a little tear, wanting to be at home with my family. I wiped it away and grabbed some Quality Street sweeties from the tin at the nurse's station to fill both my pockets. I did a few observations on the patients who were being monitored after their procedure or operation. I was then asked to go through to the opposite ward on this floor, one of the Orthopaedic wards. I was sent to cover because the staff needed their breaks and there were only two of them for nineteen patients, so I covered each of them for their thirty-minute break.

When I got onto the ward I couldn't see the staff, but I soon found them. They were in a side room with an elderly lady called Mary who had fallen out of bed and wet herself all over. She was pretty shaken up. One of the nurses, Tracey, seemed quite agitated. The other nurse, Becky, said to her 'just go on your break'.

Tracey looked so tired as she left for her break. Mary started to explain to me that she had wanted to have a poo, hence why she was trying to get out of bed and fell. She then started to shout 'Owoo it's coming' and started panicking, so we were hurriedly assisting her along towards the ensuite, but she didn't quite make it which she was very upset about. So here I was in the early hours of New Year's Day with a nurse I had never met before who couldn't even go on a break with her colleague on New Year's Eve cleaning wee and poo up from the floor of a boiling hot ensuite room. I looked up at Becky's face and she gave me a wide-eyed look and an expression that said 'For fuck's sake!', and we just cracked up laughing, Mary also started laughing from the toilet seat and we all thankfully saw the funny side, I think we might have ended up in tears otherwise, all three of us.

In situations like this, you think to yourself, 'There really must be better ways to earn money, especially on New Year's Eve/Day' but you just get on with it, and smile or laugh or you would most definitely cry.

Mary was shaken, but more upset about what had just happened because she had thought she was on the mend. We sorted her out and made her comfortable, and a cup of sweet tea and two purple Quality Street chocolates worked wonders for her. I checked her observations, which were fine, and she seemed calm, just totally mortified and embarrassed – not surprisingly considering what she had just been through. I wished I could have stayed a little longer with her just to reiterate reassurance and chat with her for a little while, but not when there are two staff for nineteen patients.

Tracey returned from her break, and then Becky went off for her break. Tracey had calmed down and had benefited from her break; neither of them had stopped since 9 pm, not even for a loo break or a quick on-the-go drink, and time was ticking on. I was in the same position and was so ready for my break! She explained why she was agitated, or rather more upset than agitated. She said they were attending to a very poorly EOL end-of-life patient, a job that needed two pairs of hands. They had a reasonably quiet spell, and all the patients were settled so they had decided to proceed with the task. She knew it would take two of them and had been asking for more staff to help and was told there wasn't any. She was upset, frustrated, and annoyed that Mary was needing their care and they couldn't give it. She used the word 'dangerous' – a word I had heard from another nurse on another shift in another place in the same week. You may ask if it was because it was the festive season, but no, as staffing problems are like this all year round. The other nurse who had used it was also agitated and had made a slight mistake with something. Again, the shift was understaffed. Both nurses were experienced professionals, but out of sheer frustration and lack of help they had become stressed, tired agitated, hungry, thirsty, and extremely close to tears.

On my return to the medical assessment unit, it was around 2 am and I still had not had a warm drink or anything to eat except a few Quality Streets. Thank you to whoever it was who gifted those Quality Streets, they had kept me going since starting at 9 pm and I was flagging. My tummy was rumbling loudly and I really needed my break, as the tiredness had started to kick in, so I asked Sister if I could take it. She apologised that it had got so late and said, of course, I could go for my half-hour break.

A break always goes quickly and because it had got so late, I sat alone in a small office without windows. I wanted to go to sleep, but at least I could wolf down my butty because I was so hungry, and no one was watching. That tuna mayo butty was the best New Year's breakfast

I have ever had! I returned with a bit more energy and was smiling and happy because we could almost see the chequered flag of home time.

At the start of the shift, I noticed another girl dressed in a white tunic like the one I was wearing. Relief and student nurses tended to wear white. She asked me if I had had a break, and I explained that I had just returned from it. She had not had hers – typical that the two agency staff were last to get their breaks.

The ward HCA told her to go and ask Sister and she said she shouldn't have to go and ask, true, but if you don't ask you don't get. I learned this not long after I joined the agency. My late Geordie father-in-law Alan taught me a good saying: 'shy bairns get nowt'.

The ward HCA said that Sister would have just forgotten to send her. I explained that I had gone and asked her, and she was sitting in the office doing her mountain of paperwork and chomping Quality Streets. I asked this girl if she was bank or agency staff. I did not know if she was a trained nurse or HCA because she had no name badge.

I got my badge made at the start of my HCA journey. It said Nicky Guttridge and Health Care Assistant under my name, it didn't cost much. I wore it proudly on my chest for all to see on every shift. I feel it avoids any confusion. At one of the private hospitals where I had worked, every one of us employed there wore a name badge and I can remember everyone's names, so it does make a difference.

Out of all the staff I worked with that night only one other nurse had a badge worn on her chest and I can remember her name – Rachael.

All trust staff have identification badges, but they tend to wear them on their hips or lower pockets or inside their pockets, making them much harder to read. I like to think all medical staff do introduce themselves before speaking to or carrying out a procedure on a patient, but I do personally like a name badge. With all the different colour uniforms and so many job titles within the big hospitals all working in different busy wards and departments, it's no wonder patients get confused as to who's who.

Dr Kate Granger started a campaign called 'Hello my name is...' in 2013. If you haven't heard of this, please take a minute to Google and have a look at Kate's story.

My husband had an eventful 'night shift' with the kids. The fireworks had woken them both up and our demanding little toddler was wanting mummy and saying he wanted daddy to go and get me in the early hours, when I was cleaning poo up. I wish Andy *could* have come and got me!

'More than half of the nurses and midwives working in the NHS in England say there are insufficient staff numbers at their trust to do their jobs properly. One-third said they have experienced work-related stress in the past year' – *Nursing Standard.*

More than half is a lot. The above quote relates to NHS trusts, and personal experience of having been employed by private hospitals. I feel if the same question were asked of private employees, it would be a very similar answer.

All the in-between shifts

My second shift for the agency was to be at a nursing home, a good thirty-five-minute drive away. It was a sunny Sunday in June, and it was a morning shift starting at half past seven and finishing at half past two, so seven hours. This nursing home was purpose-built and all on ground floor level and has about twenty bedrooms.

As I entered the home it seemed calm, probably because it was a Sunday, and I could tell straight away that I was going to like it. In many places I visited through my time employed by the nursing agency, I had a gut feeling. You just know sometimes, before you even begin to work, what kind of shift it is going to be.

We had a handover from the night nurse, and I learned that I would be working with three other members of staff, two carers, Maddison and Daisy, and a trained nurse, Jen. They were all pleasant to me from the start and made me feel welcome. How different from some of the other places I had attended. They made me feel appreciated and were thankful for my help.

The general feel of the home was a relaxed one. I was assigned to work with Maddison, who was nice and caring towards the residents. She explained everything to me, and we made a start on washing and dressing them. Daisy was liaising with the cook and seeing towards the preparation of breakfast for the residents that the night staff had already washed and dressed. Jen was sorting their medication.

Maddison and I washed and dressed two or three residents, and then I was asked to see Gertrude, a lady who was quite poorly in bed and was nearing the end of her life. I was asked to feed her again at lunchtime. She seemed to enjoy the two meals I fed to her, and I wondered if those meals would be some of her last. I think I would like to have lasagne plus chips and apple crumble with ice cream for my last meal, and a Twix chaser.

I went to catch up with Maddison. She explained that we had only got one lady left to bath, and then all the residents would be clean and comfortable, so Jen suggested that we have a quick break for some breakfast. We had a brew and some delicious toast.

We bathed Dorothy, who was new to the home and recovering from a fall that had resulted in her having to have a replacement hip. FOF, fracture of the femur, is very common in the elderly, keeping the orthopaedic surgeons busy. It was lovely to sit at the side of the bath and all three of us had a good chat and a good laugh whilst she had a good soak. The job is such an honour sometimes, especially when we do such personal tasks for our residents. There are not many other professions that get as up close and personal as us healthcare staff. She thanked us for assisting her and making her feel fresher, as she hadn't had a bath for some time, and she said it felt luxurious.

After Dorothy was made comfortable Maddison suggested that we do the toilet run. This is exactly what it sounds like - taking all the residents to the toilet before they go into the dining room for lunch. This is good working practice for caring establishments. We split into two pairs and got the residents toileted and cleaned, then placed them in the dining room ready for lunch.

You may think that taking a resident to the toilet would be quite a simple task, if you have never done it! However, when toileting residents who have been incontinent and need changing, this task can be difficult and take some time. Luckily on some occasions, you have only got to change underwear, but sometimes if wee or poo has got onto a vest or underskirt you find that you are changing almost all the resident's clothing, and if that resident is confused or suffers from dementia, they wonder why the hell you are making them take all their clothes off. For carers, tights can become a difficult obstacle when worn by an elderly incontinent resident, and stockings make our job a lot easier. You may be amazed to learn that I have rung a pair of slippers out that were that full of wee. I can still picture them – they were Scottish tartan ones. The incontinence pads catch most of it, but we do encourage drinking, so they don't go into dehydration, and that in turn produces a large output of wee.

This nursing home, in my eyes, was a good one because it was clean, tidy, and did not have a horrible smell like some places I had visited. They had everything to hand, towels, facecloths, and all the incontinence products that nursing homes should have. It is so time-consuming when you are spending most of your shift hunting for a simple thing like a towel to enable you just to do your job, and again as I described earlier, these are all hurdles when on the first shift of a new place. A simple task like going to get a towel from the laundry room can turn into quite a time-consuming job because one wrong turn could lead you in the opposite direction to the clean laundry store, then a resident might spot you and want you for something. One of the things I am very good at is directions. If I have been somewhere once I can remember how to get there again and it's the same with layouts of buildings, this really came in useful when I was being sent all over to new establishments.

After lunch was over, we moved the residents to where they wanted to be, bedroom or lounge, and made sure that they were comfortable and had everything they needed.

We then took our break and with this being a good home the residents did not tend to buzz their buzzers that often because the staff were very organised and thorough. The residents had all been toileted, fed and given their medication, so they were all contented, and most of them had their afternoon nap.

After we finished our break, Maddison and I got a bin with wheels and a lid that contained a yellow incineration bag to collect incontinence waste. We went around all the residents' rooms and emptied their individual bins of the morning's waste, I thought it was a good idea that each resident had their own individual bin for this purpose because it saved the carers trailing the waste down the corridors to the sluice. Obviously if in the morning when seeing to the resident it needed to be taken to the sluice room to be disposed of, this was done.

We also made sure that all the residents had two different colours of clean towels and facecloths to make it easier for the evening staff to carry out their jobs properly. The reason we gave two lots out was to have one set for the bottom half of their body and the other for the top. Many places use the same face cloth and towel for the bottom and face, so I did think this was a good idea, especially with some of the residents who were very incontinent.

On reflection of my second shift for the agency, I thought that this nursing home was excellent. The staff had all they needed to make the residents clean and comfortable, the staff were nice people, and the food was amazing.

I did do a few more shifts at this nursing home, and it was a one of my favourite places to work. It was a good well-run nursing home, and the free food was a huge bonus, however sadly some of the good carers had moved on because of the pay being so poor, which was such a shame.

Two agency staff at the 'dirty potato'

I was asked to work a twelve-hour night shift. These long night shifts were killers, but I always accepted them as you obviously earn more money than on a late or early shift. This nursing home was a bit far out and it took me a good 35-40 minutes to get there. At the time when you get offered the shift, you think 'Well I'd best accept as I might not get offered another if I decline it.' Beggars can't be choosers.

I had previously attended a couple of times. I arrived, followed by another agency-trained nurse, Amy, who had never been before. We had handover and then all the day staff left. We locked up the building and went downstairs to meet some of the residents who were still up. This building was a very odd shape; I don't know what kind of place it was before it was converted into a nursing home, but there were three floors, and a rickety old lift that made a right racket when in use. It reminded me of a haunted house like you see in a horror film, and the floors were extremely creaky.

Luckily there had not been too much of a gap since the last time I had worked here so I could remember some of the residents' names and where their bedrooms were. Amy and I discussed the bad planning by this home in employing two agency staff to run the place all night, especially when one had never been before. We were not worried about our capabilities; we just thought it was not fair for the residents to have two strangers to deal with.

We put the remaining residents to bed, bar one chap, Harold. He was a night owl who loved to watch telly, so we left him in the communal sitting room with a coffee and some chocolate digestives and advised him we would be back later.

Amy and I then checked and changed the others who had been put to bed earlier. In a lot of nursing homes, the residents' names are on the door and luckily for us, they were in this home, so this was helpful. We decided to do the medications together. We completed this task and most of the residents were able to tell us their names as a backup against the name on the door. After all the residents had had their medication and were tucked up for the night, we decided to join Harold and have a drink, grab the tin of chocolate digestives and have a nice rest until it was time for the next back round or a buzzer was pressed.

When we got downstairs the telly was on and there was his empty cup on the table, but no Harold. I said to Amy, 'You make us a cuppa and I'll go and see if he's gone to bed.' I remembered where his room was from the last time I attended, I didn't get in the noisy lift but ran up three flights of stairs to the top of the home – I don't think I could manage that these days! I went down the long creaky corridor to Harold's room and approached the last room on the left of the corridor, I was just about to give a gentle knock when I spotted the name tag on the door, and it said Edith. Ummm, I peeped into the room and yes Edith was fast asleep in bed, not Harold who I was expecting. Bloody hell!

It took me ages to go up and down the corridors and floors to find his name plaque on the correct door. Amy came to find me, as my cuppa was going cold. We got the giggles and were trying to be as quiet as we could wandering around the dimly lit creaky corridors, I remember it being the last door we looked at. But when we peeped into the room there was no Harold! Where the hell was he?

We slightly panicked and thought we might have to start looking in every room and disturb everyone sleeping. We knew he couldn't have gotten out of the building as we had locked up and checked the back door. Amy suggested we split up, and she went to the top floor, while I said I would start at the bottom. I got down and looked in the communal room and there he was sitting in the chair where we had left him. I ran up three flights of stairs – again – to tell Amy. We made a fresh pot of tea for us all. Harold claimed he hadn't moved from his chair; however, I saw a cheeky grin as he said it, and I think he knew exactly what he was doing.

Well, I certainly got some steps in that night shift. It

might have helped us on handover if they had said Harold and Edith had swapped rooms!

After we knew Harold was tucked up in his bed, the night went well and we did the best that we could. Another crisis staffing problem was solved thanks to two agency staff. I worked with Amy a few times in other homes, and we got on great. We lost contact with each other when I left the agency. I hope she remembers me if she reads this book.

I worked there on many occasions, on all the shift patterns. I liked the residents as most of them seemed happy and content. There was a Fanny and a Dick who lived there, and they were good friends and sat together, which always made me chuckle to myself. I do have a rude sense of humour, as I think most healthcare staff do. Certainly a lot of staff, I have worked with over all these years do, especially my Aunty Bon.

This home was run very much like Fawlty Towers. I don't think the manager was very organized and it was quite untidy and needed a deep clean. It didn't smell of wee, but it certainly smelt of something!

On one of the night shifts when I was working in the early hours, I entered the kitchen and bent down to grab a feeder cup (an elderly feeder cup is very much the same as a toddler one) to make a resident a drink. Across the kitchen I spotted a potato under the cooker. I thought 'I'll grab that later', but I totally forgot all about it until I went back a few weeks later. Again when I was grabbing a cup there it was, but this time it was sprouting all those white roots that potatoes produce. As I scrambled to grab it, I was uttering 'dirty lazy buggers' under my breath, and it went in the bin. I used to call this place the 'dirty potato'. It is not a nursing home any more; the building was turned into residential flats. I do have fond memories of my visits there as it kept me fit and made me laugh, and they always had a good stock of sweet treats.

My first hospital shift, and mental health

I will always remember my first hospital shift, which was on the ENT (Ear Nose, and Throat) ward. I was both apprehensive and nervous entering the huge NHS hospital and finding my way down to the ward. It was certainly different from attending shifts in a residential or nursing home where they always have a car park where you don't have to pay! Another payment out of their wages for so many healthcare staff.

Most NHS hospitals are vast places with pharmacies, canteens, hairdressers and shops, not to mention the hustle and bustle of umpteen different-looking staff members, visitors and patients with their drips smoking at the entrance. I think this bit may never change, even with the introduction of e-cigarettes and vapes. At every hospital up and down the country you will see at least one patient at the entrance wearing a hospital gown standing leaning on their drip or sitting in a wheelchair smoking their fag like death warmed up! It's just part of any busy hospital, just as we expect to see ambulances at the entrance.

I remember feeling confident about accepting this shift and being brave enough to give the hospital a try. As I walked in, I felt very proud to be wearing my HCA uniform and extra proud working in the big hospital of our town. Everyone knows the main hospital in the towns where they grew up, it's special, and it means something to be part of the workforce. I felt part of a huge community of fabulous staff, albeit overworked. I will remember that feeling forever.

When I arrived at the ward I had to be buzzed in. I explained who I was and which agency I worked for, and the nurse was very friendly. She showed me where to lay my belongings and asked me to come into the office and meet the other staff and have hand over. I watched as all the other staff sat down and got sheets of paper or little notebooks to begin writing their notes, and noticed that they were all trained staff except me. Thankfully I had a little notebook and pen in my pocket so I took my own notes about all the patients on the ward. There was mention of a patient having persistent epistaxis, and my face must have given away the fact that I did not know what that meant. The nurse sat next to me leaned in and whispered 'nose bleeds', and I whispered back a thank you. All the nurses seemed nice, and I was so happy inside thinking I was going to enjoy working on this ward.

Then they got around to handing over the patient in room three who I was going to be doing one-to-one with. Hmm... I had not been told about this when being booked for the shift. No wonder the nurses were being nice to me as they knew they didn't have to work alongside me! My happiness inside vanished, and I felt a bit daft for making notes on all the other patients.

This young man, Tez, had an array of mental health issues and should have been placed on one of the mental health wards, but they were all full to bursting. Because he had had some surgery to his ear nose, or throat, I can't remember which, he was given a side room on the ward.

I was given a short handover for him that explained that he was not violent to women – that was something, I suppose! He had voices in his head and the night carer had had a horrendous shift with him as he tried to throw his pillows out of the window. He wanted to keep hold of them and go out of the window as well. I looked at the clock and it was just after 7 am, so I was assigned to care for this man for six hours. I had not even met him yet and I felt anxious.

I was taken along to his room. The agency carer who had done the night shift looked extremely tired, worn out, and totally drained. She said to me 'Good luck, I hope you have a better shift than me' and almost ran out of the door as soon as I arrived to take over. The room was bedraggled and in a right state, and the floor was very sticky, which I later found out to be wee. This was my first shift in the hospital, and I thought I would be assisting the trained staff and learning all about ward work on an interesting ward.

Tez just stared at me for what seemed a long time – I think he was in a trance. The nurse said 'Just shout if you need us' and off she went to do her general nurse duties. None of the staff who worked on this ward were MH trained, and so that's where we agency workers came in useful as a lot of us had attended MH units. Tez then went on to fiddle with the bed, bedding, window, and whatever else he could get his hands on. I knew he was exhausted, like a child who fights sleep, so I talked to him softly and calmly, making up stories about all sorts of crap trying to settle him. Eventually he lay on the bed; I sat next to him and held his grubby hand and he just looked at me and smiled a sad smile. Then he settled and stared into space and drifted off to sleep. As I sat next to him holding his hand I placed the orange hospital blanket around his bony shoulders, giving him a tiny bit of comfort. I knew he had a life story to tell even though he was only in his twenties, although he looked older, as so many adults with MH do. I looked at the deep scars on both arms that had taken him onto his path to mental health and wondered if he had suffered some terrible trauma. I didn't know his story, but I knew for certain he had one and I knew it was a sad one.

My six hours dragged, but I was glad for him that he was finally getting some sleep As I sat there holding his hand whilst he slept, I appreciated my upbringing and my happy childhood.

As most people know, mental health is extremely complex and affects many children, adolescents and adults. I am so thankful for all the staff who work within mental health services. They do a fabulous job. I have massive respect for the three emergency services and the prison staff, not forgetting lots of other staff who also work within the vast array of mental health services.

I didn't let my first hospital shift put me off accepting other shifts, and I went on to work on every ward apart from maternity. My trainers had encountered lots of piss by this time and a bit of blood, sick and poo also!

After that one-to-one encounter with Tez and his complex mental health issues, I realised that adult mental health was somewhat different from the elderly health problems I was used to. I found it a little draining, if I am being honest, but I also found it interesting and I feel I gave him some comfort, so I didn't let it stop me from taking more shifts in establishments dedicated to the complexities of mental health.

I did attend quite a lot of mental health settings, even one or two secure units. I worked another New Year's Eve shift in a highly secure unit, my first shift back after my maternity leave ran out with my second child. It was different from any other place I had worked before. All staff carried bleepers and keys and I was advised about all sorts of safety measures and shown where the knife was kept in case of an attempted hanging. I was told not to enter a room with a patient. I could unlock it for them and then stand at the doorway, but never to enter the room on my own with the patient. If asked for a light for a cigarette I was shown how to hold the lighter so it could not be snatched. There were only about four or five female patients in this unit, and they were certainly outnumbered by the staff. Plus, it was New Year's Eve, so if they weren't fed up enough already for being locked up, on this evening they certainly were.

As I chatted with the registered mental health nurse in charge of our unit during the night, I learned what some of these patients had done to deserve to be locked up inside this prison-like unit. As I said, mental health is extremely complex. My family has lost someone to suicide, so I know first-hand how totally devastating mental health can be when people reach the point of taking their own life. RIP Linda x

The community hospital, and another one-to-one shift

This shift was to be at a community hospital working a night shift and it would be a one-to-one full shift. I had got used to doing these shifts and they were a good earner to be honest, but they always went slowly, although sometimes it was nice not to be running around like a headless chicken. This one was a struggle and dragged immensely. My chap, Arthur, was very confused, so much so that they had to put him in a four-bed bay on his own due to him causing havoc. He kept calling me 'lad', which was quite funny. I have had short hair for years but I have always had a distinctive bust! The trained nurse who oversaw the shift was very nice and kept popping in to check if I was ok and always brought me a drink. She relieved me to go to the loo and on a thirty-minute break. It was one of the longest nights of my career. This poor man had been in reasonable health and had just slipped into the sad decline of old age which had brought about the confusion. I finally coaxed him into taking the medication needed to calm him and at about 6 am, I think I said the captain of the ship had asked him to take these pills. He got into one of the four beds that he had been flitting in and out of all night, removing the bedding off all of them and knotting the sheets. He thought we were on a boat, so maybe he was an old sailor. I remember that shift because it dragged so much and the hours seemed to be going around extra slow as I sat watching the hands of the white clock high up on the wall tick tick-ticking away but not really moving.

I did a good few shifts here and again I was happy to go, unlike some places where I accepted the shift and then spent most of the time leading up to the date moaning and groaning to Andy about it. I must have driven him crazy whilst I was working on the agency with all my whingeing about shifts I accepted. I wish I hadn't, but you can't really be choosy when employed on the bank or agency.

My worst shift

This was to be my third shift. It was a big place with corridors like wards. When I walked in, there were staff wandering about and no one even looked at me, never mind spoke to me. I explained to someone who I was and where I had come from, and this person told me to go to the staff room and pointed me towards a flight of stairs. When I approached the top I spotted the staff toilets and a yellow door with a staff room sign attached by Blutack. I could hear laughing and voices beyond the door. When I entered the large smoke-filled room, the chatter stopped and they all looked at me. I once again explained who I was and where I was from, but no one seemed to give a shit or to know where to send me. The laughter and sarcasm of someone called Sharon were not very nice and made me feel uncomfortable. You can probably tell what my gut was saying to me at this moment.

I went to sit down and one of them said 'I wouldn't sit there, Ryan will go mad, it's his special seat,' and they all laughed. I moved.

When it was time to go on duty a lady told me to follow her. I stood to follow her and another member of staff shouted, 'is that your bag?' and when I answered yes, she said, 'I wouldn't leave it there, it won't be there when you come back,' and they all laughed yet again.

I thought, *oh my god, this place is staffed by arseholes.* I grabbed my bag and took it downstairs with me and went to put it in my car – I don't know why I didn't get in and speed away. When I returned to the door, it had a keypad which required a code, which I didn't know. I hadn't been five minutes in that place and I was upset and angry. I thought to myself, *What the hell do I do now?* Then luckily the chef came out of the kitchen and opened the door for me. He went back into the kitchen and never even looked at me or uttered a word. I just thought *jeez, what am I letting myself in for here?* The woman who had told me to follow her had vanished, and there was no one around, so I decided to walk down one of the long dingy corridors until I came across someone. I Finally came to a nurse and an office full of carers, but when I appeared at the door they all turned and looked at me as if I was an alien – no smiles, no welcome, no thanks for coming to help them out because they were short staffed.

Once again, I explained who I was and where I was from. The nurse pointed me in the right direction, so off again down another long corridor I walked. I then came across another office, and by now I was late, which was not my fault, as I had never stepped foot in this building before and not one person was willing to help me. Why should they help an agency person? I am a nice, kind-hearted person, and I would never treat anyone like this. It is mostly women that do this job who can be such bitches, it's women at their worst.

For the third time in the space of ten minutes, I explained who I was and where I was from, but still I got no nice welcome or smile. Once again, I was looked at like an alien. The nurse in charge told me to sit down whilst we had a report. It was a tiny room with no window, and they were already squashed in like sardines. No one made any effort to look at me or budge up to make room. It was horrible I felt so unwanted. I just hovered at the door like a spare part, while the night nurse carried on, finished her handover and left. I remember feeling anxious and totally isolated. I am quite amazed that each time I read this back to myself it is as if I can go back in time, because the memory is so vivid.

An older carer who was one of the cackling crew in the staff room was asked if she would work with me. I think it nearly killed her not to tut or sigh. She answered 'if I must' without even looking at me She took me out onto the corridor and said quite abruptly 'have you done this kind of work before' I answered 'yes, for years'. She said a grumpy 'good' and thrust a plastic apron at me.

We took one of the two trolleys, stacked up with sheets

and not much else, up to the top end of the corridor. This woman I had been assigned to work with had not even asked my name and she did not introduce herself. So I privately named her misery guts (MG). I tried to make polite conversation but she was just giving me one-word answers so in my head I said 'Fuck you I will never ever work with you again'.

MG explained that she was going into one resident's room and I would go into the room next door. I took the last towel and face cloth from the trolley into the resident's room. For what felt like the tenth time I explained who I was and where I was from and thankfully the resident was very nice and helpful. She made me feel slightly better as we chatted about her family whilst I assisted her with basic care.

This MG couldn't have made it any plainer that she did not want to work with me. I always found, and still do today, that working in a pair makes washing and dressing a resident much easier, especially if they need two staff to assist them with standing, which most of them did. However, people work differently. She certainly did. However, although, I felt frustrated and angry about how this MG was treating me, I had to put on my coat of thick skin and a brave face for the residents and obviously I could not express to them my disappointment with the attitudes of their staff. This first resident cheered me up. I did everything that was required and left her with the buzzer in case she needed further assistance.

I then found MG, the one I was working with. Well I say working with – I was in fact working on my own and running around the corridor looking for her when I needed help. She came back with a brew and biscuits for herself one time when I had lost her yet again. I would have loved a brew. How rude of her!

MG asked me to go into the next room and do the same again for the next resident. I checked if she had a towel and face cloth, and thankfully she did. I once again did what I had to do, wash, dress, smile, chat, and lift. I didn't bother going to look for MG after I had finished, I plodded on myself and just got on with it. I took a little bit of extra time with each person I was giving care to.

My opinion of this nursing home at the time, as you can probably guess, is unprintable. Many of the staff were young and more interested in talking about what they got up to last night than doing their jobs. The older carers were all uncouth, abrupt, rude and bitchy.

When I started working for the agency I was sent there about four times and only had one nice shift, when I worked with another agency nurse, Amy (my mate from The Dirty Potato) on a night shift.

I asked not to be sent any more - it was the second and last place I asked to be excluded from. I could cope with the places and staff that I wasn't so keen on, but the staff there were pure bitches to us agency staff.

After about a year I was asked to go back to this establishment to work 8 am till 2 pm Monday to Friday working one-to-one with a poor chap who had had a brain injury so needed twenty-four-hour care. I could not miss an opportunity to earn a week's wage, so I apprehensively agreed to do this. After the first two days, the full-time staff started to befriend me as I offered to help them a little bit, and after that week I did go back and do some shifts. Thankfully by this time they were using a lot of agency staff, as many of the bitches I had encountered had left. On a few occasions, I worked with Fred and Amy, which made the shift a bit more bearable, and I did not feel as strongly as I did when on my first few outings there as my thick skin was growing weekly and developing nicely, but it was never my favourite place to work.

I sometimes drive past this nursing home and think about my first shift there all those years ago and wonder if that horrible carer Mrs MG I worked with on that first shift is still working in healthcare. I hope not.

When I was working in the agency office word would get around that such and such place was awful and had horrid staff who treated agency staff badly, so we would have to use all our persuasive tactics to get the shifts covered. Some staff made it so obvious; some even said out loud how they hated working with agency staff. They could be bossy and rude; you just let it go over your head, kept quiet and counted the hours away. In most situations like that, I just didn't have the energy to argue, and you just know with some people you will never win.

In the early days, if I worked with horrible staff, it did of course put me off going back. In fact only a few staff members, the 'bad eggs', behaved this way and not the actual establishments – some staff even treated their own co-workers terribly. Our agency staff talked about how awful this home was to work in. We only had a handful of staff that would accept a shift there so covering their requests was not easy.

A long summer shift

I remember doing an extremely long fourteen-hour shift one beautiful summer day in a large nursing home and crying all the way home. I am a strong but also a very emotional person, as you can probably tell – I am an open book and I wear my heart on my sleeve. I love the sunshine and summer, so when I was having a bad shift and I could see a glorious day outside it always made it ten times worse, especially if I knew Andy was doing something nice with the kids. Wherever you work I think some people would agree that if the sun was shining down, you count every hour until that lovely last one comes around, especially in this country.

I was assigned to work on the top floor of this very large

home which accommodated over a hundred residents, so there were many staff. The two I worked alongside, Nicola and Lauren, had worked together over a long period of time and were close friends away from the workplace. They were reasonably nice to me and asked if I would feed breakfast to a very poorly lady who did not get out of bed. I entered the bedroom to see that there were four beds, the windows were open a little and the birds where singing. The sun was beginning to shine into the room and onto the lady, Gertrude. I drew the curtain slightly, so she wasn't squinting, introduced myself and told her I had come to give her breakfast. She just she laughed and nodded.

Gertrude had been given a wash and change and she was sitting up in bed smiling, a gappy smile as she had no teeth. She looked about a hundred years old, as she was so thin and frail. I looked down on this elderly, incontinent lady with no teeth, not much hair, so frail and scrawny looking, and thought to myself, how sad that she was living her last days in this bed. Then I looked again and changed my mind, as she was clearly well cared for. It was a nice room and she looked cute wearing her pink bed jacket. She looked comfortable, and seemed happy and just kept smiling at me. I spooned the porridge into her mouth and aided her with a cup of tea, and she loved every mouthful and every drop.

There was a family photo above her bed which looked like her grandson or granddaughter with the lady at their wedding and the bride in the photo was wearing the exact same wedding dress I had worn – what a coincidence. I said to her, 'is that your grandson or granddaughter? I had the same wedding dress'. She nodded and kept opening her mouth for the porridge, laughing at me. I liked this lady. She was like a happy little bird who loved being fed and smiled a lot, bless her. Maybe when I am heading towards the end of my days, I can think of worse places to be than a comfy bed a warm snuggly bed jacket, eating porridge and drinking tea.

After I had done this, Nicola asked if I would go and wash and dress a lady called Olive, and pointed me in the direction of her room. I walked in and nearly slipped on the poo that was all over the floor. This lady suffered from senile dementia and had a stoma, which, for those of you who don't know, is an opening formed between the colon and the tummy wall with a removable waterproof bag to collect the poo. People have stomas mainly as the result of illness or injury.

This poor confused lady had decided to remove her bag and wash it out in her sink. All she was wearing was a vest and a pair of stockings. There was watery poo everywhere, I looked at the floor, at the sink, at Olive's poo-stained vest and wanted to cry. Thankfully, as always from the experience of needing them, I had some plastic gloves in the pocket of my uniform. I began to clean the floor first, then I went to assist Olive with a clean-up, which she did not like. Being confused she got quite agitated and started lashing out at me with her poo-covered hands, which made this awful task even worse. I remember the sunshine beaming into this quite large bedroom and thinking to myself 'there must be better ways to earn money'.

When Olive and her room were clean, I thought it would be a good idea if I brought her out of her bedroom, so I sat her in the communal sitting room, where we could keep a closer eye on her. I explained to Nicola why I had been so long, and the reply was 'oh she does that all the time, she will probably do it again today at some point'. I looked around this locked sitting room and thought to myself 'this is so sad'. There was a television in the corner with Richard and Judy chatting away and no one watching it. There were two other ladies in this locked room. One was wandering around looking like a zombie and the other woman was sitting in a reclining chair just shouting out words that did not make sense. There was a table in the other corner with nothing on it - if ornaments or cutlery were left in this room they would just be destroyed by these poor confused souls. In the lovely nursing home where I met my beasties, we had a resident called Joyce, and when we took her to her room to get her ready for bed, we would find all sorts about her person, a salt or pepper pot in her cardigan pockets and loads of things stuffed down her incontinence pad, teaspoons, forks, napkins, ornaments. We used to say to her 'what are we going to discover today, Joyce?'

Some carers and nurses love working with confused residents. I didn't mind, but at times it made me quite sad, and I found it made my job a lot harder than it already was. Many residents with dementia can walk miles and miles in the course of a day. Some mutter gibberish all day long and when you have a room full of people all shouting continually it gets draining. When it comes to taking them to the toilet, these poor people hang on to their clothes as tightly as they possibly can and look at you as if you are going to hurt them. On some occasions, you struggle to pull their pants down to sit them on the toilet and they pull them back up as fast as you're trying to pull them down.

They need baby bibs at mealtimes in order to protect their clothing whilst they eat, and as soon as you turn around, they have taken them off. They strip naked and walk around as if they are on a nudist beach, something they would have never done in the days when they were of sound mind. It is emotionally hard for their family members as they have long forgotten the strong bond that was once so special to them.

I don't really remember much more about that shift except that it was one of the warmest days ever, and the well-deserved cold cider in the garden when I got home was like nectar.

A bitchy nurse

I was persuaded to return to a particular nursing home and do a day shift from 7 am to 5 pm. I accepted and then spent the rest of the time until setting off moaning and groaning at myself for agreeing to do it, because I was slightly anxious about this particular nursing home. This was because the last time I had attended and worked the night shift, I had made the hard decision to report a staff member, as I described earlier. The thought of working with this woman again filled me with dread. I had not realized how upset and anxious this 'bad egg' had made me until that moment of getting out of my car. My palms were sweating and my heart was beating. It is amazing how just one person can make you feel. I have spoken to my friends about how bullying within the workplace can affect people and unfortunately, it happens more than we think in many places.

As I was walking towards the entrance, I was saying in my head over and over, 'Please don't let her be on duty'. The person in charge asked me to go along and work on team two. I had worked there a lot and knew the layout of team two, so that was a bonus for me. She explained that I would be working with a young girl called Ashleigh, and the relief I felt when I knew I didn't have to go upstairs lifted my mood instantly. However, the next hurdle was that the 'bad egg' was going to be on duty. I entered the room, and she was nowhere to be seen. I felt myself breathe a sigh of relief. I enquired about her and was told she had moved on. Good for me and the residents here, but not for the place she had moved to.

I asked Ashleigh what she wanted me to do. There were four of us altogether working on team two, and I stayed with Ashleigh while the two other staff members worked together. I worked well with Ashleigh and the two other staff were nice to me. This helps immensely. It is really upsetting when the person you are working with is being funny and awkward with you. It did make me wonder sometimes in this kind of job, where we are all supposed to be caring and kind. I can and do stick up for myself, but it's far easier to just get on with people.

After working with the now reported 'bad egg' on the previous shift there I had made a promise to myself that I was not going to let anyone upset me as she had done and vowed to stand up for myself the next time someone made a snide comment or was not being nice to me or the person being cared for.

We had finished the morning's work and the residents were sitting at the tables ready for lunch. Anyone who has done the job know exactly how hard the work is, so when the team work well together and get all the morning tasks done before lunchtime is a good feeling, as it doesn't happen very often.

The radio was playing, and Ashleigh was folding

napkins. I asked her if there was anything she wanted me to do and she replied that everything was done, and we were just waiting for lunches to be brought along to us in the bain marie (warming device on wheels) by one of the kitchen staff. I sat down on the edge of a settee and the nurse who oversaw our team came along with the medication trolley. It was her job to dish out the lunchtime medication to the residents.

She walked in, no smile, looked at me sitting on the edge of the chair, and said to Ashleigh 'Look at her, I wish I could sit down all morning'. I was flabbergasted. I could not believe that she had just said this because she had popped along a few times and had seen us working hard all morning, I thought, *right, it's now or never*. Feeling quite nervous, I stood up and walked over to her and said 'sorry, what did you just say?'

I could tell she wasn't expecting this, and she said she was joking. I said in a calm voice that I had not been sitting there all morning, that she had seen us working and that if she had any task she wanted me to complete for her she only had to ask. I kept my nerve and cool and went on to say that I would be happy to do any task required and asked if she wanted me to assist her with the meds.

I think the fact that I had answered her back had shocked her and I had caught her off guard. She looked at Ashleigh and asked her if anything needed doing. Ashleigh explained that because we had worked hard all morning we were ahead of time and were just waiting for the lunches to arrive as kitchen staff arrived with the trolley. With this I felt the woman was embarrassed, as her cheeks flushed a little. She locked her meds trolley and disappeared. I felt proud for sticking up for myself, especially to the person in charge. I was so chuffed that Ashleigh stuck up for me as well and she gave me a smile that said, 'Good for you'.

The bitchy nurse arrived again after ten minutes to give medication to the residents, and when lunch was nearly over she asked me if I would like to go to the lunch break with Ashleigh. I said yes and thanked her, and she said she would help clear up and we were to have an extra five minutes.

As I said before, women at their worst!

Residential homes

Some care staff may argue that rest homes can be a lot easier than working in a nursing home due to a large majority of residents not needing nursing tasks. My view of this is that any care job is hard work in different ways. The residents may be slightly fitter but that leaves more time for cleaning, doing laundry, mopping ironing, peeling and chopping the lorryloads of vegetables that are needed for the next day.

In many places the manager is a trained nurse and is always on call when not on duty. Residential homes have senior carers who have completed their NVQs and can dispense pre-packed blister pack medication to the residents and deal with any problems that may arise. District nurses come into the homes to attend to any dressings, stomas, catheters or bloods that need to be taken.

I worked in one rest home that took me less than ten minutes to get to, so I was always pleased when these shifts came up as it was the nearest establishment to my home. It was a lovely friendly cosy place, but I felt that there were too many rules and regulations that spoilt things.

I was working a night shift one night and assisted a gentleman upstairs to his bedroom to help him get ready for bed. A carer followed us upstairs with something he had forgotten. This gentleman had all his faculties. I asked him if he wanted a wash now or in the morning and he replied 'in the morning'. The man did not have food on his face or hands. I gave this man a choice about having a wash because I feel quite strongly about patient choice, and I also feel that so much choice is taken away from them once they enter a home.

The carer said, 'oh don't be naughty, you know you have a wash before you get into bed'. I looked at him and pulled a face behind her back and started to fill the sink up with hot water. He smiled and rolled his eyes and after she left the room he said, 'Make it a quick cat lick'. We laughed. I sometimes go to bed without having a wash. You might think that's dirty of me, but it's my choice. I didn't challenge her as it was her workplace, not mine.

This lovely chap and I had a good old chat about all sorts. He had worked at a well-known place in Lancashire where a lot of men from his era had worked and was telling me all about his life. I loved that aspect of the work. I find the older generation so interesting as they lived in a totally different time from me, so their stories are so intriguing to hear. There is always something to be learned by spending a bit of time chatting with elderly folks.

In many places, the carers even take away the residents' freedom to choose what clothes they will wear the next day and will get the clothes out for the morning when they put the resident into bed. I remember a young carer asking me what dress we should put on a resident one morning and I simply replied, 'Let's ask her'. Don't get me wrong – if the resident can no longer make that choice, then this is fine, but just think about it – we all have our favourite clothes and our comfy ones. Just imagine if someone else chose your clothes for you!

In every caring establishment I have ever worked in. At 6 am it's like the start of a marathon – they are in so much of a rush. Many night care assistants begin washing and dressing residents then or even earlier, in order to get a certain number of residents up and dressed so the day staff won't moan about the night staff being lazy. For years I worked day and night shifts, and of course, the night shifts are in some ways easier as sometimes the residents sleep, but there are still tasks to complete. Days may seem harder as it's noisier with more people coming and going. It's a rare establishment where there is no bitchiness between day and night staff, and between upstairs and downstairs staff.

A little rest home – and the sleepy resident

I worked in one rest home on a night shift where there were only sixteen residents. It was a nice little home, but one thing that spoiled it was the fact that on some occasions the staff began washing and dressing residents before 6 am in order to get nearly all of them up for the day staff. To me, this is wrong. I did both day and night shifts at this home, and it was not hard work compared to other places I had visited the staff here didn't know they were born compared to the HCAs who worked in the larger establishments, but they thought they were overworked.

I remember one occasion when I did a night shift with Clare, and she said at about 5 am, 'Right, shall we make a start?. It is very hard for an agency carer to say, 'Hold on a moment, this is not on', So I just said, 'Bloody hell, isn't it a bit early?' She did look a bit embarrassed, and she held back until around 5.45. I followed her into a bedroom shared by two ladies who suffered from Alzheimer's. Clare pointed to one of the sleeping residents and said, 'Right, you do her and I'll do her'. This resident woke with no problem, and she began to wash her. The resident who she assigned to me was fast asleep, so I pulled the covers back and started to repeat her name. I felt very awkward and in a terrible position having to take my orders from Clare, as I was just there to help. This lady did not want to wake up and looked so cosy and snug. Years afterwards this still makes me so cross and it still upsets me when I think about it.

I looked across at Clare, who was by now well on her way with washing and dressing her resident. She made no attempt to make eye contact, so I stood my ground and explained that I was not prepared to wake this resident up. I checked if her incontinence pad was soiled but it was not; if it had been and she had had a wet or dirty incontinence pad on I might have been able to justify to myself waking this poor woman up and getting her out of bed. Clare by now had her resident practically dressed, and I had not even got my resident to sit on the edge of the bed. I thought Clare must be thinking, 'I wish she would make a start'. I explained to her that I was not going to do this as in my eyes it was abuse, and said I would go and look upstairs and see if another resident was awake or soiled. I would not feel as guilty about dragging them out of their bed at six a.m.

I knew Clare was totally pissed off with me. She did not have to say anything, as her face said it all. But I did not care about her annoyance as I was so cross with her.

I began to think about the two strong independent much-loved women in my life who had shaped me and always stood up for me, Grandma, who passed away aged eighty-five, and Nana, who lived to be ninety-seven. They were my family, my grandparents, who had worked hard over the years, and they were the reason why I always treated other residents with love and respect as they are other people's loved ones. So bloody well let them have a lie in, they have earned it.

I went upstairs and looked around for an awake resident. I followed the smell of poo, and it took me to Barbara's room. I told her I was going to give her a nice wash and get her up and dressed ready for some breakfast and she said yes; she did not even realise that she had been incontinent. I began to fill the sink up with water, but it was stone cold. The bedrooms at this place were tiny. I told her not to worry and that I would come back in a moment, but she began to get upset and said, 'Don't leave me', so before I could go and get the things I needed I had to calm this lady down. I knew that because this was a rest home it was not as well equipped as a nursing home, and it did not even have a sluice.

I was not prepared to wash this lady with cold water, I went downstairs for some hot water from the kitchen, then carried it upstairs in a jug. I put my gloves on and made a start. It was very time-consuming because after I had cleaned up her dirty bottom half up, I had to go downstairs for more hot water to wash her top half. I wanted to put her in a bath, but I couldn't manage this on my own and decided not to ask Clare as I knew what her answer would be.

Each time I went downstairs to get the hot water I noticed that there were more and more residents up and dressed, all sitting around in the lounge slumped asleep in their chairs. The lady whom Clare had assigned me to wash and dress was one of them. When I saw that, I was blazing inside and wanted to shout at her, 'How can you fucking justify doing that to an old lady?' But as always it is easier to think it than say it.

I eventually got my resident up and dressed, sorted the dirty bed linen out and took her downstairs. By now it was about 7.30. I came across Clare, who was sweating and looked like she wanted to punch me in the face. I tried to explain what had happened and why I had been so long, but she made it quite clear that she was angry with me and walked off. I managed to get another resident washed, shaved (a job that many carers leave till later), and dressed before I left at 8 am.

There was one resident for the day staff to wash and dress. I would have bet my wages that Clare had slagged me off to the day staff and portrayed herself as the good worker, having got all the residents up and dressed and me the bad worker, having got only two residents done, but as I was driving home I thought to myself that at least the two residents I had got up in the morning had been washed with warm water, not cold. I went home to bed with a clear conscience. But as I said, that shift will stay with me forever, because it made me so sad to think of that lady who just wanted to sleep.

Another shift I worked at this home was on a Sunday, so it was a nice, relaxed day. My shift was a full day, working from eight a.m. to six p.m. When we had done all the morning tasks and lunch was over the lady in charge, Ali, explained that all the residents were clean and comfortable and many were having their afternoon forty winks. It was about 2 pm. There were only the three of us on duty, so we decided to take our break together, and sat in the office adjacent to the communal sitting area.

As we were sitting there, a relative of one of the residents whom they had been visiting came back into the building to tell us that one of our confused residents had escaped through the kitchen door and gone off for a wander. We all went running out and found the visitor's husband with the resident on the back doorstep. We brought her back inside and thanked the visitors. They looked less than impressed, and rightly so, as they had every right to look disappointed. The chef had left the door open while he nipped home for his break, and this resident, who suffered from dementia, had wandered out through it. The three of us all felt dreadful, although in hindsight, after any incident or accident, there are always ifs and buts.

We should have made sure the door was locked, or Mr. Chef certainly should have. He got a stern word in his ear from Ali on his return. I felt embarrassed in front of the visitors who found her, and I also felt we had let the lady down who was in our care. Although accidents happen, I do feel that this one could have been prevented.

Inexperienced care staff

I was asked to work a night shift at another small residential home where I had worked on many occasions. I had worked on every shift, early, late, full day and night, so I had got to know many staff and residents. I arrived at work knowing from my past experience that there would be just the two of us. One benefit of working for the agency was that I was never placed in charge.

I went into the office for the handover and was introduced to Nina, who I was going to be working with. I had not met her before. She seemed nice but a little up tight. She explained to me that she had never been placed in charge before and portrayed herself to be very apprehensive and annoyed. I tried to reassure her that we would be fine and if there were any problems we would just ring the on-call person.

Once the day staff had gone, she explained to me why she was annoyed. She had never done this kind of work prior to working here and had only just got the job two weeks ago, which was why I had not met her before. Also, she had not been advised that she would be in charge until she arrived. I did feel that this was slightly crafty of the home. The situation Nina had been placed in was unfair due to the simple fact that she was not ready to have that responsibility. Being thrown in at the deep end happens a lot. I think most of us have had it done to us many times.

We worked well together throughout the night and I kept reassuring her and helping with all the tasks required of us. I found that in many establishments when there are staff shortages the people in charge will do almost anything to get staff to commit to a shift, even if it involves putting them at risk. I use the term 'risk' because I feel that this home did put Nina, and unfortunately their residents, at risk, because she was inexperienced in the line of work never mind being in charge.

I remember working another 'risky' night shift at one of the large residential homes and feeling terrible because a patient had buzzed her bell to ask for some pain relief as she was experiencing a lot of pain in her back, but we couldn't give her any because the senior carer had gone home after dispensing the bedtime medication. If it was up to me I would have rung her to come back and get some medication for this lady. It was not up to me though, so it was left until a senior came on duty in the morning! Another sad tale of the consequences of staff shortages.

At one of the above establishments, there was a very

old blind lady, Margaret, who reached 103 years old before she passed on (I read about her death in the local newspaper). She did not like going to bed because she was frightened on her own. Maybe the blindness scared her? The care staff would pop her into bed, and she would spend hours shouting and getting upset. Her family gave permission for her to stay downstairs, so she would sleep in the sitting room in a comfortable recliner chair with her thick tartan rugs wrapped around her. The staff said she was comforted by the noise of them doing their jobs.

One night whilst on duty I was given the task of vacuuming and dusting the sitting room and Margaret was in her chair wrapped up fast asleep. How she could sleep with the noise of the Hoover going always made me smile. I was busy Hoovering up and before I knew it, I had got one of Margaret's orange tassels caught in the Hoover. By stepping on the rug and pulling the Hoover back I finally retrieved it and had to laugh because she never moved. She must have been in a deep sleep, or maybe that was the night she passed away and I didn't notice! RIP Margaret. Only joking, of course, I would have noticed if she had died.

A hard shift – and a lazy nurse

I did a night shift at one home which for me was a 30-minute drive away. It was to be an eleven-hour shift and I had never been before. I arrived at the establishment to find that it was a very large purpose-built home. It amazed me to find bathrooms in purpose-built homes that were so small you couldn't swing a cat in them. It was obvious that the designers had never struggled with a resident plus a wheelchair, a hoist, etc. whilst trying to toilet them.

I introduced myself when I arrived and was asked to work on the middle floor. I climbed the stairs thinking that the home was tastefully decorated and furnished. This group owns quite a few establishments, and they are all very similar inside and out. I found the nurses' station and introduced myself to the two trained nurses who were sitting there. They said hello and introduced themselves and we started to hand over. I thought there must only be two of us on this floor for the night duty, but then another care assistant arrived, a bit late. As we worked together, I learned that her name was Amanda and she was one of the kindest, most caring, gentle people I ever worked with. She was a single mum who had had a terrible life struggling on a shit carer's wage, and I was telling her to go to do her nurse training. I really hope she did because she was worth so much more. But I never saw her again because that night shift was the one and only time I went there. I must have worked with so many staff and given care to so many people over my time at the agency, these numbers would be huge if I could have counted them all.

After we had handover the trained nurse began to do her medicine round. There were a lot of poorly residents who were tube fed, so she would see to these throughout the night. I went with Amanda, and we began to do a back round – it should be called 'break your back round' in some places. There were about thirty residents, and Amanda explained that nearly all the residents on that floor suffered from dementia, and a few were bed bound and tube-fed. All the residents were in bed except one man who was zipping around in his electric wheelchair. When I spoke to him it was clear that he was slightly confused. He knew Amanda's name and he knew where his bedroom was, but I noticed that he had been incontinent when I saw the large wet patch soaking his lap. Amanda explained that he could become very aggressive towards the staff and she asked him if he wanted to go to bed. He said no, so I asked him if he would like to get ready for bed and again he replied no. I thought if this gentleman's family came in to visit him they would see that he had been incontinent and perhaps think that we were not very good staff, because we had left him wet, or maybe they knew that he could become aggressive, I didn't know. As agency staff, we do not get to form bonds with any relatives.

Amanda suggested that we would leave him for now and try again when we completed our round. We started at one end of the corridor. The first room we entered had two beds but only one resident. It smelled of poo *and* wee, and the light was on in the en suite. I turned the light on in the main bedroom. but it didn't work. Let's hope it had been reported and was on a to-do list!

We struggled to pull the divan bed away from the wall because during the night when you are changing residents it makes it easier when you can walk down either side of the bed. I got to the stage where I started to hate divan beds because most of them are pushed up against the wall, and when you are dealing with a resident that requires two carers. In most cases it means pulling the bed away from the wall, which can pull on your back. I think a lot of places push the bed up against the wall because the rooms are too small to have the bed in the middle of the room and most places will not have enough cot sides. I have worked in hospitals with beds that can be pumped up so that nurses and carers are not bending whilst attending to a patient. In hospital, the staff pump the beds up whilst making them. It makes you more aware of how much you are bending and pulling when working with divan beds.

We found that this lady had been 'rooting', a term that many carers and nurses use to describe when a resident has been scratching or poking their bottoms, so she had poo all over the place, on her face, hands, her night-dress, and all over the cot side. I walked over to the en suite to get a bowl of water and Amanda shouted, "Watch out!" I had almost stood in a large dollop of poop this lady had thrown out of her bed onto the floor. We just started laughing. As I said before, sometimes if you didn't laugh you would cry. It was Friday night, 10 pm, hotter than hell, I had just started a long night shift and I was already nearly standing in poo!

We cleaned and changed this lady and went on to the next room. With this floor catering mostly to residents with dementia, we found that nearly all the residents had been 'rooting', so it took us a lot longer to do our back round. The two of us were basically clearing wee and poo solidly for about three hours. I ask you to try it, bending over divan beds, not many cleaning cloths, confused residents, with pooey hands trying to grab us for three hours solid – let me tell you, it is bloody awful. We deserve medals. I could have drunk a gallon of something, as you get so hot and thirsty.

The trained nurse who was on duty with us had now finished giving the medication out and when I went to answer a buzzer, she was sitting with her feet up reading a magazine with a cup of tea, can you believe that? I was gobsmacked. Amanda explained that she never helped the care staff, ever!

We still had about ten residents to see to and she did not even come and see if we were ok, check how we were getting on, or offer us any help. How can someone do that? I certainly couldn't.

Chapter 6

Time to leave it all behind

The main reason why I changed my career path was the years of lifting without not using the correct aids, bending and twisting my back on most shifts. It certainly took its toll and over the years, I suffered a good few slipped discs and time off sick with back pain. I have had X-rays, an MRI scan, physiotherapy, chiropractors, a podiatrist, and many back massages. I was at one time considering getting shares in ibuprofen and paracetamol! Then I had a Pars Defect stress fracture in my lumbar spine and moved on to taking strong medication. I truly believe that being a carer for all those years was the cause of this. I know a high percentage of healthcare staff suffer from back pain and agree with what I have just said. Luckily for me, the MRI scan didn't show any major damage.

I have been working since I was 14 years old, and I have never skived off or lied about being sick. I realised a long time back that all of us who are employed are only ever numbers in the workplace. Some staff can be much better than others, some are happy to help and go above and beyond. However, we are all still a number – if we leave, they replace you in a heartbeat, so put yourself and your family first, go home on time and only do extra if you really want to. If work starts making you ill, don't be afraid to move on. Most of us are employed for a long time, so you need to be happy in your employment.

From my time being employed by the agency, I found that the turnover of staff was high. Lots of people try it, but it takes a hardened few to stick with it for a fair few years as I did. I hope I have not put you off if you are thinking about joining an agency because since my time, there have been many changes for the better and there are good points to consider, like the money and the flexibility.

If you have ever worked as a relief staff member, whether with an agency, locum, or bank, you may have read this book with a slight smile on your face because you will be able to totally relate with me and probably connect with many of the situations I have talked about. I'd love to hear some of your stories.

If you are healthcare staff and have worked with relief staff, I would just like to ask you to take a minute to think about how hard it is sometimes for us *good*, experienced agency staff to do our jobs.

I feel that very few healthcare staff will never have had a bank or agency carer work alongside them, and I just want you to think about it the next time you work with one. Please try and be nice, because remember we are only there to help, and it really does make a massive difference to us when you are pleasant. I do understand the frustration surrounding the pay issue and realise that this is probably the main reason that other staff treat us badly at times. I am also aware that there are many lazy relief carers, but in many cases, they haven't got the experience and have been basically chucked in at the deep end. Some of these people will become wonderful relief staff with experience.

I also feel that many staff who have done the job for years can get a bit complacent and forget that residents are people. I have seen staff treat residents like something on a conveyor belt – wash, dress, undress, lift, and on to the next resident, as if they are trying to win a race.

Thankfully I have plenty of common sense and a very good sense of direction, a good sense of humour and a thick skin. This helped me get by, especially when I was working for the nursing agency. For example when you cannot find a clean towel, you know that they cannot be too far away so I used to look behind doors. Most times I would find a towel or whatever it was that I needed to carry out the job that I was doing.

In all the years that I have worked as an HCA things have changed enormously, especially with policies, procedures, and regulations. I do think that the introduction of DBS – the Disclosure and Barring Service – is a good thing.

Employers can check for a criminal record before deciding to employ people to work with vulnerable adults or children. The television programmes that have been made over the years do not change. The ones showing undercover workers exposing horrendous working conditions, with staff who have become whistle-blowers, are always very interesting, but there is always another one to be made the year after.

One whistle-blower story was that of Margaret Haywood, a nurse for over twenty years. The Nursing Medical Council struck her off the register because she voiced her concerns and, according to her, was ignored. She said, 'It makes me ashamed of my profession'. You can see her interview on YouTube. There are other stories of nurses whistle-blowing and being suspended and or sacked, leading to the end of their career. No wonder staff think very carefully before blowing that whistle. Freedom to Speak Up came to fruition in February 2015, when Sir Robert Francis published his Freedom to Speak Up report, an independent review into creating an open and honest reporting culture in the NHS. There are many Freedom to Speak Up Guardians employed within NHS establishments.

Even though it is a well-known fact that agency staff get paid more money than some regular staff members that they are working alongside. I sure as hell wouldn't have done it for less. I deserved every penny I earned, and no one could ever excuse me of being a lazybones. This was why managers used to ask for me personally to cover some of their shifts, which always made me feel appreciated.

Another thing that I used to appreciate was a simple thank you. It's lovely when a team leader says a personal thank you for your time – it really does make you feel that you have helped.

It is inevitable that things change as the years come and go, and the top bosses try to find solutions to the ever-increasing problems that will always arise within the healthcare industry.

I would love to see all these bosses don uniforms and just actually work one shift, then see what changes they would implement. Recently Ed Balls, the broadcaster and former politician, did just that and he has gone up in my estimation as a result.

I remember working with a trained nurse at a private hospital and cringing at the unprofessional way she dealt with a busy morning. Other staff members did not gel with her; she was just one of those people who are hard work to get along with. We have all worked with people like that in our careers. There were four of us working a very busy night shift. At 6 am a gentleman arrived to be admitted for an operation that morning, and the day staff did not start until 7 am. Fiona started complaining and saying 'I can't be doing with this, we're the night staff, I'm seeing to these patients, I'm not admitting him, he will have to wait for god's sake' or words to that effect. This patient overheard all this as Fiona stormed off. Someone apologised for her behaviour and said she was very tired. He did not look very impressed. We all have a moan and a groan, but most of us have some decorum and don't do it within earshot of patients or the person you're bitching about.

There was a change in tactics a few years ago. Many owners of healthcare establishments suddenly realised that they could cut the cost of their relief staff bills by using staff from abroad. As part of their contract, accommodation was provided, but their pay was even less than they gave their own staff, and this stopped them from calling the agencies for extra cover. It was certainly a strain for agency proprietors. When I first started in the agency office, we used to have pages upon pages of shifts to cover from the establishments. However, it then went full circle because the overseas staff got homesick and realised they were being treated unfairly, so they returned home. Consequently, the banks and agencies picked up business again.

No one is perfect and we all make a mistake or two along the way. I made a mistake one day. During handover it is commonplace to make a note of any allergies the patient may have. One particular woman had an allergy to apricots and the nurse handing over to us said jokingly 'So don't be giving her any apricots'. We all laughed, because it would be extraordinary if we ever had apricots to offer the patients. After breakfast had been served, I was collecting the trays and noticed a patient had not eaten her yogurt, so I said, 'Do you want to keep hold of your yogurt for later?' and she said it was apricot flavour and she was allergic.

I had a mortifying moment on my first-ever shift at one of the private hospitals. I was so nervous I knocked a glass of water all over a patient in bed after he had had surgery, so we had to get him up out of bed, change all the sheets and put him back in. I'm actually cringing as I think about how embarrassed I felt at that time.

Another time, first shift at a new place, I had just arrived for a night shift and was asked to go and shut all the windows in the rooms along the corridor I went through a door at the end of the corridor because I saw a window open on the landing, then turned around to go back through the door, but it had locked and had keypad entry. It took ages for them to find me, although I was knocking like mad.

I worked all the way through the Covid-19 pandemic, which will be talked about for years to come, even though a lot of us who worked through it might want to forget it all. Just listen to a few podcasts from the front-line medical staff and you might understand just how truly awful it was working at the forefront of it all. I had the first Covid vaccination at 12 noon and was working the afternoon shift in the huge vaccination centre. I was proud to be part of the NHS administration team who worked right through the pandemic, but at times it was very stressful.

For example, we had to get to grips with learning a brand-new computer data entry system that none of us were used to, while coping with people's emotions, staff and patients. It just pissed us healthcare staff off when we heard people saying they had booked the day/ week off work just in case they had a reaction! Sitting on their comfy settees watching 'homes under the hammer!

Before I sign off, I would ask you all to please speak with your family members about Advance Care Planning, which is basically what it says on the tin. Doctors' surgeries should have a leaflet or someone to speak to about your final months, weeks or days. If you do not have a will, make it a priority to get one, and make a list of your wishes. Do *you* want to be resuscitated? (DNACPR – Do Not Attempt Cardiopulmonary Resuscitation).

I have seen a very frail ninety-five-year-old being resuscitated because the family wanted her to stay alive. She had said to us more than once she was ready to die but had never mentioned death or dying to her loved ones so as not to upset them, so she got pounded instead of passing peacefully when she was ready to go and took to her grave a couple of broken ribs from being so frail. Families can become very selfish in situations when a loved one is dying or has died. Write it all down and sign and date it. I have seen neighbours falling out over the television of a deceased lady who had no family in a nursing home I kid you not, a fucking television! Her bed was still warm.

Family members who once got on fine sometimes don't speak after a fallout when a loved one passes away. Inheritance money is stolen from other relatives. Houses we have worked hard for have to be sold to pay for our end-of-life care. Spend it now – you can't take it with you. It's a hard discussion and none of us really want to think about the ends of our lives, but getting everything in order eases the process for you and your loved ones when making the final arrangements. Pick your songs and your vol-au-vents, or give all your money to the cat's home if you want to, just make your wishes known to your loved ones.

There will always be the need for relief staff and there will always be the need for shifts to be covered by them.

I have seen many poems written about nursing and caring over the years. There were a lot to choose from, and I have chosen the two below. When I saw the first one for the first time it hit me with its truthful, powerful words. I have seen it on notice boards in many establishments, so many people may have read it. It is said that this poem was found in the hospital locker of an elderly lady after her death.

Look closer, see me!

What do you see nurses, what do you see?
What are you thinking when you look at me?
A crabbed old woman, not very wise,
Uncertain of habit with faraway eyes
Who dribbles her food and makes no reply

When you say in a loud voice, I do wish you'd try!
Who seems not to notice the things that you do?
And is forever losing a stocking or shoe.
Who resisting or not, lets you do as you will
With bathing and feeding, to long day to fill.
Is that what you're thinking, is that what you see.
Then open your eyes, nurse, you're looking at me.
I'll tell you who I am as I sit here so still.
As I move at your bidding, eat at your will…
I'm a small child of ten with father and mother.
Brothers and sisters who love one another.
A young girl of sixteen with wings on her feet,
Dreaming that soon a love she will meet.
A bride of twenty, my heart gives a leap.
Remembering the vows that I promised to keep,
At twenty-five now I have young of my own
Who needs me to build a secure, happy home.
A woman of thirty, my young now grow fast
Bound together with ties that should last.
At forty, my young sons have grown up and gone,
But my man's beside me to see I don't mourn.
At fifty, once more babies play round my knee,
Again, we know children my loved one and me.
Dark days are upon me, my husband is dead.
I look to the future; I shudder with dread.
For my young are all rearing young of their own,
And I think of the years and the love that I've known.

I'm an old woman now and nature is cruel,
Tis her jest to make old age look like a fool.
The body it crumbles, grace and vigour depart,
There is a stone where I once had a heart.
But inside this old carcass a young girl still dwells,
And now and again, my embittered heart swells
I remember the joys, I remember the pain.
And I'm loving and living life over again,
I think of the years, all too few, gone too fast,
And accept the stark fact that nothing can last.
So, open your eyes, nurse, open and see.
Not a crabbed old woman
Look closer – SEE ME!

I'm fine, thank you

I'm fine thank you,
There is nothing the matter with me.
I'm as healthy as I can be.
I have arthritis in both my knees
And when I talk, I talk with a wheeze.
My pulse is weak, and my blood is thin,
But I'm awfully well for the shape I'm in.
Arch supports I have for my feet,
Or I wouldn't be able to be on the street,
Sleep is denied me night after night,
But every morning I find I'm all right.
My memory is failing, my heads in a spin,

But I'm awfully well for the shape I'm in.
The moral is this as my tale I unfold
That for you and me who are growing old
It's better to say 'I'm fine' with a grin
Than to let folks know the shape we are in.
How do I know that my youth is all spent?
Well, my 'get up and go' has got up and went.
But I really don't mind when I think with a grin
Of all the grand places my 'get up' has been.
Old age is goldened I've heard it said
But sometimes I wonder as I get into bed
With my ears in the draw, my teeth in a cup
My eyes on the table until I wake up
Here sleep overtakes me.
I say to myself.
'Is anything else I could lay on the shelf?'
When I was young my slippers were red
I could kick my heels over my head.
When I was older my slippers were blue,
But still, I could dance the whole night through.
Now I am old my slippers are black
I walk to the store and puff my way back.
I get up each morning and dust off my wits
And pick up the papers and read the obits.
If my name is still missing, I know I'm not dead,
So, I have a good breakfast and go back to bed.

- Constance O'Neon

* 9 7 8 1 8 6 1 5 1 1 3 4 8 *

BV - #0100 - 110324 - C0 - 203/127/11 - PB - 9781861511348 - Gloss Lamination